This book is dedicated to the memory of all the suffragettes and suffragists who did right and persisted knowing Failure was Impossible.

Consultant: June Purvis, Emeritus Professor of Women's and Gender History at the University of Portsmouth

The author would like to thank
Suzanne Carnell, Lynn Roberts Maloney, June Purvis,
Chris Inns, Becky Chilcott, Helen Weir, Anita Anand, Lauren Laverne,
Jenny Shone, Ros Ball, Regina Marxer and Chris Williams
for their help, guidance and involvement in the making of this book.

First published 2018 by Two Hoots
an imprint of Pan Macmillan
20 New Wharf Road, London N1 9RR
Associated companies throughout the world
www.panmacmillan.com
ISBN 978-1-5098-3967-4

3 5 7 9 8 6 4 2

A CIP catalogue record for this book is available from the British Library.

Printed in China

The illustrations in this book were created using watercolour,
ink and graphite pencil on hot press paper.

www.twohootsbooks.com

SUFFRAGETTE

THE BATTLE FOR EQUALITY

David Roberts

WOMEN DEMAND THE VOTE

TWO HOOTS

Courage calls to courage everywhere,
and its voice cannot be denied.

MILLICENT GARRETT FAWCETT

CONTENTS

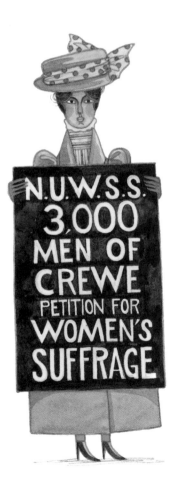

Foreword

WHEN I WAS GROWING UP IN NORTHEAST ENGLAND IN THE 1980s, I DIDN'T HEAR A LOT ABOUT THE SUFFRAGETTES.

If you'd asked me to name one, I'm quite sure Winifred Banks, the mother from the film *Mary Poppins*, would have been the only name I could call to mind – and to be honest, I wasn't all that keen on her. With her upper-class accent, fancy clothes and a giant house that looked like a wedding cake (it literally contained a magical nanny to look after her children while she went off on suffragette marches), she was nothing like any of the mothers I knew. In *Mary Poppins*, Mrs Banks is portrayed as a rather spoilt, distracted, neglectful wife and mother, busily and selfishly devoted to a cause that is invisible and seems irrelevant to those closest to her.

I didn't know then that this was an entirely typical (and typically inaccurate) depiction of the women who – over one hundred years ago – risked so much to fight for the right to vote. I didn't realize how cruelly unfair Victorian society was to women and girls. (I didn't realize how unfair the society I was growing up in was to women and girls either, but that's another story.)

The book in your hands is an introduction to some of the people who fought to change that, and succeeded. They were quite unlike Winifred Banks. Whereas she was spoilt, they were willing to use whatever privileges they had to fight for equality (check out Princess Sophia Duleep Singh in the chapter 'The Rebel Princess').

Mrs Banks was posh, and although some of the real suffragettes were posh too, many came from other backgrounds and did all sorts of different jobs, which helped them win the vote in the end (as you'll read in the chapter 'Canaries and Penguins Help Win the War').

Mrs Banks came across as a bit wet, but the suffragettes were tough: like Edith Garrud – a ju-jitsu expert and leader of suffragette bodyguards the Amazons – and the many others who suffered the torture of force-feeding while in prison for their protests. Mrs Banks seemed to pay little attention to her children, but the suffragette movement was led by one of the most famous mother–daughter dynasties in British history, the Pankhursts.

In the early 1990s, when I was a teenager, feminism was still unfashionable. But then, the feminist punk-music movement riot grrrl came along. Its empowering message, songs and visual language – slogans, badges, banners and home-printed 'fanzines' – captured my imagination. I started a band with friends, and it changed our lives.

I wish I had understood sooner that the call to use our voices had reached us using the very tools the campaigners of the women's suffrage movement pioneered. They too had badges and slogans – including 'Votes for Women', 'Deeds, Not Words' and 'Dare to Be Free' – which they displayed on banners. They too published their own newspapers, including *The Suffragette*, *Votes for Women* and *The Vote*: anything to spread the word and attract more supporters.

The women in this book may be illustrations, but they are not caricatures. They were real and complicated. We remember them as winners, but they often failed. Their victories were rarely glorious – more often they were gradual, small or compromised. They argued passionately for their cause, but sometimes fought among themselves. They made mistakes. Their views were opposed by some of the most important people in the country (plenty of whom were women themselves).

We look back at the lives of the women (and men) of the women's suffrage movement knowing that they would win their fight and that history would show their cause was just, but they had no guarantee of this at the time. One of the many lessons they can teach us is that this is precisely what progress looks like when you're in the middle of making it happen – unlikely, slow, messy, complicated and imperfect. They can teach us that it's OK for people to be those things sometimes, too.

Enjoy this beautiful book. I hope it inspires you to do your imperfect best to make the world a better place.

Lauren Laverne

Introduction

UNTIL I WAS FOURTEEN YEARS OLD, I HAD NEVER HEARD OF THE SUFFRAGETTES.

The year was 1984 and my history teacher, Mrs Pile, informed the class that for our end-of-year exam we had to write and illustrate a project on a topic we had studied during the year. Had I heard right? Illustrate! I was thrilled: anything that meant I could draw was a bonus.

A collection of faded old history books on a variety of subjects was scattered on the teacher's desk, and one by one we each went up to choose a book on which to base our project. Amid the books about Humphry Davy, Edward Jenner and Isambard Kingdom Brunel was a book that caught my eye. It had a black-and-white photograph on the cover showing two women in prison uniform: dark dresses covered in white arrows, aprons tied around their waists, mop caps on their heads. They stood arm in arm and above them the title read *The Suffragettes*.

Who were these people? What was a 'suffragette'? And what terrible crime had they committed that they had been sent to prison? I took the book eagerly and turned straight to the bit in the middle where the pictures were. Slowly the story revealed itself.

These were Edwardian ladies of the early 1900s who had protested and battled with the government of their day to win 'the Vote'. They had smashed stuff up, burned stuff down and even died to be given equal political rights with men. I was captivated. Their struggle for equality really spoke to me.

Most of my friends were girls, but I am sure back then not many of them would have called themselves feminists. Being a teenage boy, I certainly didn't realize

I could call *myself* a feminist. But I had a very strong sense of injustice at the way boys and girls were treated differently.

In those days, the gender divide was still very stark: at school, boys played football, girls played netball; girls did needlework, boys did metalwork. Why? I would have been much more at home in the needlework class than doing metalwork, and I know that some of my female friends longed to be on the football team. But those options just weren't available to us, or if they were, not many people would want to stand out by choosing them.

The expectation for boys and girls to fit into their gender stereotypes seemed to me ridiculous, and so unfair. One friend of mine who did proudly call herself a feminist would always speak out if she felt she was being dismissed, stereotyped or patronized because she was a girl, but often her protest was met with groans from teachers and pupils alike.

Our class at school had never studied the suffragettes in history, or in any other lesson for that matter, so I have no idea why that book was on the teacher's desk. It's a mystery. But it started in me a lifelong interest and respect for this group of women who had stood up to the men in power and begun to change the way society viewed their gender and the way it restricted their lives, ambitions and right to be seen as equal citizens with each other and with men.

More than thirty years after I wrote my school project, I have delved back into it and learned so much more about the campaign for women's suffrage. Of course, illustrating this book has been enormous fun, researching amid the treasure trove of newspaper reports, photographs, posters and postcards that the Internet has made readily available. I have interpreted some of these images to make my own illustrations, and have enjoyed visualizing scenes from some of the stories I've read for which there were no photographs.

Stories like Mary Leigh hurling slates off a rooftop at the Prime Minister's car in Birmingham. Or Miss Spark and Miss Shaw barricading themselves in at the top of the Monument tower in London in order to unfurl a massive banner that read 'Death or Victory' before showering the astounded crowds below with hundreds of pamphlets declaring 'Votes for Women'. Or the fearless Muriel Matters being pelted with rotten fish as she gave a speech in front of a rowdy crowd of men.

I am not an expert, more of an enthusiast, inspired by a diverse group of people, both suffragists and suffragettes, courageous, determined, peaceful and militant, all focused on one thing: the right to vote.

One hundred years since women first won the right to vote, we continue to challenge ourselves on gender equality and the expectations and roles of women and men. Slowly we chip away at the limitations and barriers to equality that previous generations, and many people still today, suffered and suffer. Femininity does not equal weakness, and gender equality benefits everyone.

The campaigners for women's suffrage understood that. Here are some of their extraordinary stories.

David Roberts

A Man's World

SO WHY WEREN'T WOMEN ALLOWED TO VOTE? IT'S SAD TO SAY, BUT THROUGHOUT HISTORY, BOTH IN THE UK AND IN MANY OTHER PLACES AROUND THE WORLD, WOMEN AND GIRLS WERE THOUGHT OF AS BEING WEAK AND EVEN A BIT SILLY, CAPABLE ONLY OF BRINGING UP CHILDREN AND BEING GOOD HOUSEWIVES.

A woman wasn't considered capable of making major decisions even about her own life, and certainly not about the way the country should be governed. Men were expected to make those decisions. Men were expected to be in charge. So men took control and made all the rules. Often the rules they made favoured other men who were just like them, however unfair that might be. For instance, even by the mid-nineteenth century, the Victorians didn't bother to educate girls the same way they would educate boys. Some girls would have had some sort of education, but only if they were rich, and either went to a private girls' school or had a governess to teach them at home. Education was expensive, and a path to a profession, a career and an intellectual mind: the things a *boy* needed to get on in life, and not considered the concern of girls.

In 1870, a law was passed that made school free. In 1880, schooling was made compulsory up to the age of ten, then eleven in 1893, and fourteen in 1899. But this did not represent as much progress for girls as you might think. Girls were often kept at home on washdays or other days to help around the house. And it is not just going to school but what is being taught there that matters. In addition to reading, writing and arithmetic, girls traditionally learned cookery, needle-work and general domestic duties: all great skills, but if these subjects are seen as 'girl only' subjects, then it is clear that a girl is being trained to be no more than a good housewife, while the boys are being encouraged to expand their minds and prepare for adult life beyond the home.

As time moved on, girls' education did get better, but progress was frustratingly slow. University places for women were rare, and even if she did get a place to study a subject like medicine or law, which for a man might become his profession, a woman wouldn't be allowed to work as a doctor or a lawyer after she graduated. Women weren't allowed to be doctors until 1876, or lawyers until 1922.

But university was in any case out of reach for most people, women or men: only the wealthy could afford it.

For most of the population, life was tough. Men and women worked long hours as servants or in factories, down mines or as farm labourers. The work was not only hard, it was often dangerous, and pay was low.

To make matters worse for women, their pay was even lower than that of men. A woman could not expect to be paid the same wage as a man, even if they were doing the same job. And most often she still had to go home after a hard day's work and clean the house and cook the meal.

But unequal pay, an issue for many even today, was just one of many shocking inequalities for women at this time.

If a woman got married, she had to promise to 'obey' her husband in her marriage vows, but a man never had to promise to obey his wife. Being married meant she gave up what few rights she did have as a single woman: a wife was 'owned' by her husband. He also owned all her wealth and property. Even if the home they lived in together had belonged to her before she got married, her husband could boot her out on the street without a penny if he wanted to divorce her. She, on the other hand, could not even divorce him without his agreement.

A woman had no legal rights over her own children until 1839, when a law was passed to give a woman the right to apply for custody (or guardianship) of her children if they were under the age of seven. The same law also gave her the right to apply for access to her children over the age of seven. Before this, if a marriage broke down, a father could take his children away from their mother and legally deny her the right to ever see them again.

Thankfully, many people realized these laws were wrong, and by the end of the nineteenth century lots of the worst old laws that discriminated against women had gone. Women were gradually gaining more control over their lives.

Yet still they were not equal citizens with men. They were not allowed to vote in parliamentary elections. Some men thought this was the way things should stay. Most surprisingly, some women thought so too.

But by the time the Victorian era ended with the death of the Queen in 1901, one group of people had been for many years asking the question: why can't women vote? Recognizing that nothing would change fundamentally for women until they could take part in elections, they began to demand that the government give them the vote. These people were called 'suffragists'.

What is Suffrage?

'SUFFRAGIST' IS THE NAME GIVEN TO SOMEONE WHO CAMPAIGNS FOR THE RIGHT TO VOTE, EITHER FOR THEMSELVES OR FOR OTHERS.

If you yourself have the right to vote, you can still be called a suffragist if you believe that other people who don't have it should have a vote too.

'Suffragist' comes from the word 'suffrage', which means the right to vote in political elections. The right to vote is sometimes also called the 'franchise'.

Using your franchise, or voting, is important because it is a way of expressing your choice or point of view when a decision is being made on which a group of people have different opinions. A democracy is a system of government in which everyone should have an equal right to express their point of view.

The United Kingdom today is a democracy. At least every five years, there is a parliamentary election called a general election. Everyone over the age of eighteen is asked to vote for a Member of Parliament (MP). Everyone is free to vote for an MP who they think will best represent their point of view in Parliament on the big decisions about how we live our lives. Some people believe that the voting age should be reduced, but there is no longer any distinction between men and women or rich and poor.

Things were not always done this way. Throughout history (and still today in some places), people have had to fight and struggle to be given the right to vote on equal terms with others.

For a very long time in the United Kingdom, women were not allowed to vote in parliamentary elections and so women had no say in how the country was governed. They had no way of expressing a political view or of influencing the laws under which they lived. They were denied suffrage.

It was indeed a man's world … but not for all men equally. It wasn't a simple case that all men could vote and no women could. For many years, millions of men were also denied the right to vote. It took a long time, many riots, violence and petitions to the government before things started to change.

To better understand the story, we need to travel back in time to the Middle Ages.

VOTES FOR WIMMEN

VOTES FOR WIMMEN

A woman's place is in the home

Centuries ago, the country was ruled by the king, and he alone made decisions for the people. But the king needed the support of the noblemen and landowners who paid him taxes, and over time these men decided that they should have a say in how the country was run.

This eventually led to the creation of a permanent parliament in which the noblemen voted and made the laws.

Most people living in Britain were not noblemen; they were ordinary working people. And they had no vote.

So all the decisions about how most people lived their lives were being made by a very small, privileged group. This was not full democracy.

As time passed, many of the 'ordinary' people, fed up with such injustice, demanded their right to a vote as well.

A huge change happened in 1832, when a decision was made in Parliament to allow some more men to vote. This was called the Great People's Reform Act, but although it was a step in the right direction, it only allowed more wealthy men to vote and still excluded millions of other men – and all women.

I will be your leader some day

By 1867, more and more people were demanding suffrage. A decision was made to give men who owned their own homes the right to vote. This was the Second People's Reform Act, but it still excluded many working men – and all women.

By 1884, the fight for universal suffrage was growing even stronger. The government passed the Third People's Reform Act, giving many more men the right to a parliamentary vote, but it still excluded millions of working-class men – and all women.

Some MPs tried to persuade the Prime Minister, William Gladstone, to give women the vote. But although he was not entirely against the idea, he believed there was not enough support in Parliament, and that the law would not be passed at all if women were included.

Gladstone was probably right. Queen Victoria herself wrote to him, cautioning against this 'mad folly of women's rights', a view still commonly held at the time.

But the suffragists were not about to give up, and the campaign for votes for women was getting steadily more powerful.

1832: The Vote Lost

BUT WAIT! HAD SOME WOMEN BEEN ALLOWED TO VOTE, MANY YEARS AGO?

Some suffragists believed they had, and that in their campaign for votes for women they were fighting not for something new, but for something that had been taken from them.

It was known that long ago in Anglo-Saxon England, an abbess (the woman in charge of an abbey) had been involved in law-making. St Hild of Whitby was a very powerful abbess. She founded an abbey that was home to both nuns and monks. Historical documents showed that St Hild had been engaged in the politics of her time, involved in discussions with the king in the year 664 about when Easter should be set in the calendar year.

Politicians writing down this new law in 1832 used the words 'male persons' to indicate who was now allowed to vote. Previously the word used was 'mankind', a word often used in laws and understood to describe both men and women.

In 1867 a clerical error did add one woman's name to the electoral register: Lily Maxwell, a Manchester shopkeeper.

When it came to the attention of the local suffrage groups that Lily had been accidentally registered to vote, they made sure she did just that, and on 26 November 1867 Lily Maxwell became the first woman to vote in a parliamentary election since the law had changed in 1832.

Her pioneering action prompted over 5,000 women who owned property in and around the Manchester area to try and register their names on the electoral roll in 1868. All of them were rejected.

Some suffragists also believed that later, in Tudor times (the 1500s), women in England who owned land had voted in parliamentary elections.

If that is true, then it means the right to vote was taken away from women by the introduction of the Great People's Reform Act.

But the fight for women's suffrage was beginning in earnest. A fight that was to last another sixty years before women would be able to vote on equal terms with men.

1832–1897: The Acorn Becomes a Mighty Oak

WOMEN HAVE BEEN STRIVING FOR EQUAL RIGHTS WITH MEN FOR HUNDREDS OF YEARS, BUT BY 1832 STILL VERY FEW PEOPLE, MEN OR WOMEN, WERE IN FAVOUR OF GIVING WOMEN THE RIGHT TO VOTE IN PARLIAMENTARY ELECTIONS.

But one person who did think it important decided to write a petition to Parliament. Her name was Mary Smith and she lived in Yorkshire.

A petition is like a letter to the government asking them to do something. Mary pointed out that as a woman she had to live by the exact same laws as men and pay taxes just as men did, so why should she not be able to vote, just as men did? Without a vote, she had no influence over either laws or taxes, which was completely unfair. Most MPs thought this was just a bit of a joke, and in 1832 no one took Mary seriously at all.

In 1866, a group of women called the Kensington Society, who also thought it very unfair that women had no vote, decided to write their own petition. They included Barbara Bodichon, Emily Davies and Elizabeth Garrett. They had friends who were MPs: John Stuart Mill and Henry Fawcett, both of whom supported votes for women. John agreed to take the petition to Parliament.

If you want to get your petition noticed, you need people to sign it – lots of people. The Kensington Society's petition had 1,499 signatures of women, rich and poor, from all across the UK. Teachers, dressmakers, shopkeepers, scientists, mathematicians, servants, as well as lots of very posh ladies, all signed it. But the government took no notice.

Imagine how frustrated those women must have felt when only a year later the law changed to give 938,427 more men the vote – but still no women.

In 1867, the Kensington Society became the London Society for Women's Suffrage. This was the beginning of a properly organized women's suffrage movement. Soon more and more societies appeared up and down the country.

This did not amuse Queen Victoria, who in 1870 declared, 'Let women be what God intended, a Helpmate for Man.' But this only made the suffragists even more determined to win.

In 1897, seventeen suffrage societies joined up to make one big group called the National Union of Women's Suffrage Societies (NUWSS). Their first president was a very wise and powerful woman called Millicent Garrett Fawcett.

Millicent Garrett Fawcett

MILLICENT FAWCETT WAS BORN IN 1847. BACK THEN HER NAME WAS MILLICENT GARRETT, AND SHE WAS ONE OF TEN CHILDREN.

As a girl, Millicent enjoyed reading books and learning, and was sent to boarding school in London. As she grew up, she became very interested in the education of girls and women, and how unequally they were treated compared to boys and men. For example, her older sister, Elizabeth Garrett (later Garrett Anderson), had found it difficult to find a college where she could study to become a doctor, just because she was a woman. (But Elizabeth didn't give up, and went on to become Britain's first female doctor.)

Another of her sisters, Louise, introduced Millicent to lots of interesting people who had forward-thinking views on women's rights. In 1865 they went to hear a speech given by the MP John Stuart Mill. Millicent was captivated by his progressive ideas and belief that women should have equal rights with men. This was a shocking view to hold at the time.

In 1867 Millicent married the MP Henry Fawcett, himself an avid supporter of women's rights. Henry was blind, and Millicent would act as his eyes by writing out speeches and debates that took place in Parliament.

She spent many hours sitting in the Ladies' Gallery, the part of the House of Commons where women were allowed to go to watch the proceedings. She didn't much like the Ladies' Gallery. It was hot and stuffy and gave her a headache. But by now Millicent had a keen interest in politics herself, and wrote books and essays on the subject.

She became an outstanding person in the campaign to win votes for women, and although she didn't much like public speaking (in fact it made her feel sick), she gave many speeches, not only about votes for women, but also on education and the rights of working women. Millicent knew that if women gained the vote, it would be a stepping-stone towards changing many of the terrible ways they were being treated in the home and the workplace.

As the leader of the NUWSS, the biggest of all the women's suffrage societies, she insisted that its members campaigned peacefully, within the law, but relentlessly. She always maintained this was the only way to achieve public and government support to win the vote.

When women finally won full equal voting rights with men, Millicent had been peacefully campaigning for sixty-one years.

MARY SMITH

From Yorkshire, in 1832 she was the first woman to petition the government for the right to vote, arguing that since women paid taxes to the government, they should be allowed to vote for it.

ELIZABETH WOLSTONHOLME-ELMY (1833–1918)

A campaigner for girls' education, a member of the Kensington Society and later member of the WSPU, on marriage she refused to 'obey' in her vows, to wear a ring or to give up her surname.

LYDIA BECKER (1827–1890)

An amateur scientist interested in botany and astronomy, she founded the *Women's Suffrage Journal*. She was Secretary of the Manchester National Society for Women and an NUWSS leader.

JOHN STUART MILL (1806–1873)

A politician and campaigner for gender equality, he was the first MP to call for giving women the vote. He is now perhaps best known as a philosopher who believed in the importance of individual liberty.

Suffragists and Their Supporters

SUPPORTERS OF WOMEN'S SUFFRAGE FORMED MANY GROUPS, UNIONS AND FEDERATIONS, MOST OF WHICH WERE NON-VIOLENT, UNLIKE THE MORE MILITANT ACTIVISTS OF THE WSPU.

Eighteen of these groups joined forces to create the biggest women's suffrage organization, the NUWSS. Known as suffragists, their tactics were different from those of the WSPU, and focused on campaigning within the law. By 1914 their more restrained style had attracted about 55,000 members to join the union once described as 'a glacier, slow moving but unstoppable'.

But not all the suffragist groups acted within the law. The Men's Political Union for Women's Enfranchisement (MPU) and the Women's Franchise League (WFL) both had militant activists among their members, including window smashers and those who refused to pay taxes.

HUGH FRANKLIN (1889–1962)
A member of the Men's and Jewish Leagues for Women's Suffrage, he was a militant activist, imprisoned and force-fed 114 times. He married fellow WSPU member Elsie Duval, sister of Victor.

CHARLOTTE DESPARD (1844–1939)
A novelist, a founder of the Women's Freedom League, and of the Irish Women's Franchise League, she was a pacifist who encouraged militant protest and was imprisoned more than once.

VICTOR DUVAL (1885–1945)
Husband to the suffragette Una Dugdale, he founded the militant Men's Political Union for Women's Enfranchisement and was a member of the International Women's Franchise Club.

CATHERINE IMPEY (1847?–1862)
A Quaker, vegetarian and women's suffrage supporter from Somerset, she founded Britain's first anti-racist journal, *Anti-Caste*, and arranged for a British lecture tour by US civil rights campaigner Ida B. Wells.

HENRY FAWCETT (1833–1884)
A politician, he was husband to Millicent Garrett Fawcett and one of the earliest campaigners for women's rights. He was blinded in a shooting accident at the age of twenty-five.

MURIEL MATTERS (1877–1969)
Australian born, she was a member of the Women's Freedom League, famous for her fearless publicity stunts. A journalist, lecturer, actress and educator, she stood for Parliament in 1924.

WILLIAM BALL
With jobs ranging from gardener to master tailor, he was one of the few men to become a militant activist. A window smasher and often imprisoned, he was force-fed over one hundred times.

TERESA BILLINGTON-GREIG (1877–1964)
A teacher, journalist and writer of books on women's rights, she was a key organizer of the WFL and frequently imprisoned. She and husband Frederick Greig joined their surnames on marriage.

1903: The Time Is Now

ALTHOUGH THE MOVEMENT HAD GROWN, BY 1903 THE SUFFRAGISTS' PROGRESS WAS SLOW, AND ONE GROUP GREW INCREASINGLY IMPATIENT FOR CHANGE.

Some campaigners, like Millicent Fawcett and members of the NUWSS, continued to lobby the government peacefully to give women the vote by organizing petitions and encouraging MPs sympathetic to their cause to raise the subject in Parliament. But some of the women, frustrated with the government's refusal to listen to them, felt ignored and overlooked. It was time for a defiant new voice to speak up. Emmeline Pankhurst had had enough of talking, which she felt was achieving nothing.

One evening in October 1903 at her home in Manchester, along with her eldest daughter, Christabel, and some like-minded local women, Emmeline formed a new women's suffrage group, the Women's Social and Political Union (WSPU). Anyone could join . . . as long as they were female. Unlike the NUWSS, no men were allowed to join as members, although they were welcome as supporters.

Men like Frederick Pethick-Lawrence. His wife, Emmeline, was a member of the WSPU and became Honorary Treasurer in 1906. Frederick and Emmeline both believed in equality between men and women and even took each other's names in marriage. So Emmeline Pethick and Frederick Lawrence became Mr and Mrs Pethick-Lawrence, which made a very clear stand against the idea that a man 'owned' his wife.

The Pethick-Lawrences later worked together as the editors of the WSPU's newspaper, *Votes for Women*, which was launched in 1907. By 1910 the circulation had risen to 30,000. It was being sold throughout the country, both through newsagents and by individual members of the WSPU, who often stood in the gutter to do so, since standing on the pavement could be called an obstruction and might lead to their arrest. It was an excellent campaigning tool, spreading the message of the fight for women's suffrage through cartoons and articles, by advertising forthcoming meetings and demonstrations, and by reporting on the activities of WSPU members. It was a rallying cry to supporters and called for new members to join up.

As a barrister, Frederick Pethick-Lawrence also represented the WSPU in legal matters, including trials, because women were not allowed to do so. Christabel Pankhurst had a first-class honours degree in law, but because she was a woman, she was not able to work as a lawyer.

Christabel became the key strategist of the WSPU, and she and her mother, Emmeline, set out the broad outlines of policy for the union. Individual members had considerable freedom to decide which acts they should engage in, be it working at headquarters, taking part in protests or just giving money to the WSPU; but the leaders set the tone.

Right from the start, the WSPU saw itself as an army, and its members as soldiers, working together. All that was required was an unquestioning loyalty to the cause.

Many women liked this new bold approach and were attracted to the active spirit of the Union. The WSPU's membership quickly swelled to become an impressive fighting machine, a force to be reckoned with, led by the determined Emmeline Pankhurst.

Emmeline Pankhurst

BORN IN 1858, EMMELINE PANKHURST LEARNED ABOUT POLITICS FROM A VERY YOUNG AGE.

As a child, Emmeline Goulden (as she then was) would read newspapers aloud to her father and, school bag in hand, accompany her mother to women's suffrage meetings. Both her parents held strong views in favour of women's rights.

She went to school in Manchester, and later in Paris, but Emmeline realized that her education was never taken as seriously as that of her brothers. Theirs focused on business, mathematics, science – subjects a boy could build a career on – whereas hers focused on domestic skills, teaching her how to keep the home nice and care for her family. Emmeline was indignant: why should she be expected to keep the home nice for her brothers, while they were never expected to do the same for her?

One night, she overheard her father whisper to her mother, 'What a pity she wasn't born a lad.' Emmeline wanted to shout out in protest, 'I don't want to be a boy!' But from then on she realized that the world saw men as superior to women – and became increasingly determined to change that view.

In 1879 she married a lawyer, Dr Richard Pankhurst, who was himself a radical thinker and strong supporter of women's rights. She became very interested in the lives of working-class women, and in 1888 lent her enthusiastic support to the 'Match Girl Strikes'.

The match girls and women worked up to fourteen hours a day in a factory making safety matches. They were on very poor pay, and could be fined for something as minor as talking, or even for going to the toilet without permission. In addition, they suffered from very poor health because of the chemical, phosphorus, used to make the matches. It made their skin turn bright yellow, and their hair fall out, but worse still, it gave them a hideous bone-rotting disease called 'phossy jaw'.

When the story of these truly appalling working conditions reached the newspapers, first in an article written by the campaigner Annie Besant, the factory bosses tried to force the women to sign a statement saying the reports were nonsense and that in fact they were all having a lovely time at work. Some refused to sign, and when the leader of that group was sacked, 1,400 women and girls walked out on strike. The strike lasted three weeks, but by the time the women returned to work, their demands for better working conditions, including no more fines, were granted.

Emmeline saw just how powerful women could be by standing together to fight for their rights, and this spirit inspired her in the formation of the WSPU and throughout her days of campaigning.

Deeds No

1903

The first thing Emmeline Pankhurst and the leaders of the brand-new WSPU did was to come up with the brilliant slogan 'Deeds, not words.'

A phrase that would encourage and motivate; a rallying cry to women everywhere that the time for politely talking about votes for women was over. Now was the time for action! Time to get the job done. Emmeline Pankhurst said, 'Women don't want to be law-breakers, they want to be law-makers!' But break the law they would.

1905: 'The Question! The Question! Answer the Question!'

IT HAD ALL GONE A BIT QUIET BY 1905. MOST PEOPLE, INCLUDING THE NEWSPAPERS, WERE NOT PAYING MUCH ATTENTION TO THE WOMEN'S SUFFRAGE CAMPAIGN. BUT THAT WAS ABOUT TO CHANGE.

The government at the time was Conservative, and their main opposition was the Liberal Party. Campaigning had begun for the 1906 general election, and the Liberals planned a meeting at the Free Trade Hall, Manchester, where MP Sir Edward Grey would speak, and answer questions from the public.

Christabel Pankhurst and fellow WSPU member Annie Kenney decided to go to the meeting. They made a large banner that read, 'Will the Liberal Party Give Votes for Women?' which they intended to let down from an upper gallery during the meeting. But they could not get seats in the gallery and had to change their plan at the last moment. They needed something smaller to wave, so cut down the large banner to just three words: 'Votes for Women'. This slogan would go on to be used around the world.

They waited until a few men had asked questions and been answered before Annie Kenney stood up and asked in a calm voice, 'If the Liberal Party is returned to power, will they take steps to give votes to women?'

At the same time, Christabel waved the small 'Votes for Women' banner. There were gasps and shouts of disbelief that a woman would dare to speak out in this way. Annie was forced back into her seat, while a man held his hat over her face to shut her up.

When the rumpus had died down, Christabel shouted out the same question, which again resulted in much shouting and heckling from the crowd. In the face of such disorder, the meeting was brought to an abrupt end, but the two women were not about to be ignored. They shouted again and again, 'The question! The question! Answer the question!'

The crowd became angry, attacking Christabel and Annie, who were dragged out and flung on to the street. Passers-by stopped to see what all the fuss was about, and Annie and Christabel were arrested for causing an obstruction. Christabel was also charged with assaulting a police officer by spitting in his face after her ejection from the Hall.

The two women were given a choice between a fine and a prison sentence. Both chose prison, saying, 'We will get our question answered, or sleep in prison tonight.'

The WSPU vowed to disrupt all Liberal Party meetings from then on, until their question was answered.

1906: Bang, Bang on the Door

THE PRESS REPORTS OF WHAT HAD HAPPENED AT MANCHESTER'S FREE TRADE HALL IN 1905 SPREAD OUTRAGE THROUGHOUT THE COUNTRY.

The arrest of Christabel Pankhurst and Annie Kenney made headlines everywhere. Some people were horrified by the women's behaviour; others were horrified by how the authorities had treated them. But their act of civil disobedience energized a new interest in the campaign.

Civil disobedience means deliberately refusing to obey the government. It is a way of protesting against certain laws to draw attention to an issue. After 1905 it became the chief weapon of the WSPU.

As more and more women joined in the heckling and disrupting of political meetings and rallies, the newspapers really started to take notice. There were reports of women being arrested for repeatedly knocking on the door of Number 10, for jumping on the Prime Minister's car, and for chaining themselves to the railings of government buildings and even of Buckingham Palace.

The WSPU were finding new ways of attracting publicity, and Number 10 Downing Street was to become a frequent target throughout the campaign.

In 1909, Daisy Solomon and Elspeth McLellan tried to deliver a message personally to the Prime Minister by posting themselves to him. At this time Post Office regulations allowed individuals to be 'posted', so the two women paid to have themselves 'delivered' to Downing Street by a telegraph messenger boy. The butler who came to the door refused to sign for the 'human letters' and eventually they were returned to the offices of the WSPU. But not before the press had taken photographs, ready for the next day's newspapers.

Society was scandalized by such reports: this was not the behaviour expected of respectable ladies. But it showed just how determined members of the WSPU were to win. The government continued to ignore these campaigners, dismissing them as hysterical shrieking women. But they were not about to give up.

Some of the other suffragist societies got very annoyed with the WSPU, claiming its militant actions were damaging their own tactics of persistent, law-abiding lobbying of the government.

But it was too late. Civil disobedience was getting gradually more extreme. And the newspapers loved it.

1906: Rotten Fish and Bad Eggs

I N A TIME WITH NO TELEVISION, NO INTERNET, NO MOBILE TELEPHONES OR EVEN NATIONAL RADIO BROADCASTS, IN ORDER TO REACH A LOT OF PEOPLE, PUBLIC SPEECHES WERE ESSENTIAL.

The suffragists and the suffragettes gave a great many speeches so that people could hear what they wanted and why they wanted it. The speeches might be to hundreds of factory workers at the end of their working day, when the speaker had to climb on to a cart or a chair to be seen above the assembled crowds outside the factory gates. Or they might be to thousands of people at grand gatherings in parks or squares in towns and cities. In London's Trafalgar Square, the speakers stood high on the plinth of one of the famous lion statues. Journalists stood in front of them, writing down what they said to print in the newspapers, so that even more people would hear the message.

When a speech was due to be given, signs would be chalked on to walls and pavements, with the names of who would be speaking and at what time, and with arrows directing people where to go.

This meant that troublemakers also knew where to go, and they would turn up to disrupt and intimidate the speakers, who were an easy target for abuse. The speakers were sometimes pelted with oranges or worse, or shot at by naughty children with pea-shooters. Some speakers would wear heavy mackintoshes (waterproof coats) to protect themselves against all the rotten fish and bad eggs that would be hurled their way, and they were often jeered at and heckled by an angry crowd shouting, 'Down with suffragettes!', 'Go back home and mind the babies!', and even, 'Throw them in the river!'

But nothing stopped them speaking. They just carried on regardless, so that thousands of women and men got to hear about the fight for equal rights. As a result, many joined suffrage societies, growing the membership to create a stronger force ready to stand up to the government.

The campaign reached all corners of society, from the wealthiest to the poorest, with speakers coming from all classes. Working women, even less used to speaking in public than those from the middle or upper classes, were given lessons in public speaking. They were encouraged to give speeches not only to working-class women who knew very well the hardships of a working life, but also to middle-class and wealthy women's groups. They told stories from personal experience about life with low pay and poor working conditions, to remind the rich of just how important it was to include *all* women's needs in the demand for equal rights. They were campaigning not only for the vote itself, but for wide social reform in all walks of life.

1906: '–ette'

AS THE ACTIONS OF THE WSPU GREW MORE DARING, JOURNALISTS BEGAN TO TAKE MORE INTEREST. ONE OF THESE WAS CHARLES E. HANDS OF THE LONDON *DAILY MAIL*.

In a report on the disruptive behaviour of the WSPU in 1906, he changed the word 'suffragist' to 'suffragette' to distinguish the militant members of the WSPU from the more peaceful, law-abiding members of the other suffrage societies.

There was a fashion to add '–ette' to the ends of words to describe things as small, inferior or feminine (which in the eyes of many people at the time amounted to the same thing). So a small kitchen would become a kitchenette; a short book might be called a novelette; and a cheap substitute for leather made of paper or cloth was called leatherette. By replacing the '–ist' at the end of 'suffragist'

with '–ette', it made the word seem insignificant, small, silly, or fake. To call the militant members of the WSPU 'suffragettes' was mocking and making fun of them, like a bully calling you a bad name.

But something strange happened. Instead of being upset or angry about being called 'suffragettes', the

WSPU members reclaimed the word, proudly using it to describe themselves. They said that 'Suffragists "jist" want the vote, but us Suffragettes intend to "get" it.'

The WSPU recognized that the term 'suffragette' would catch the attention of the general public – which is exactly what they wanted. In 1912, they named their second newspaper *The Suffragette* (which changed to *Britannia* at the outbreak of war in 1914).

The word 'suffragette' was only used to describe members of the WSPU, who were all women, whereas 'suffragist' was used for any woman or man campaigning for votes for women both in the UK and elsewhere in the world.

But although their strategies might differ, both suffragettes and suffragists were equally determined to win their fight for votes for women on the same terms as men.

ANNIE KENNEY (1879–1953)
The only working-class woman to be part of the WSPU hierarchy, she worked in a cotton mill from the age of ten, where she lost a finger in an accident. She was imprisoned and force-fed many times.

VERA 'JACK' HOLME (1881–1973)
Chauffeur to the WSPU leaders, she was a member of the Actresses Franchise League, which staged women's suffrage plays. She became an ambulance driver in the First World War.

SYLVIA PANKHURST (1882–1960)
An artist, she designed many of the WSPU's posters and banners. She was imprisoned and force-fed many times. During the First World War, she helped open four mother and baby clinics.

MARION WALLACE-DUNLOP (1864–1942)
A sculptor and book illustrator, when she was imprisoned for throwing stones through the windows of Number 10 Downing Street, she was the first person to go on hunger strike.

Notable Suffragettes

From princesses to seamstresses, the bold spirit of the WSPU attracted nearly 8,000 women to sign up and join the fight for political equality. Some of them resorted to violence to catch the attention of the public, press and government. Over one thousand went to prison where hundreds joined the hunger strike and were forcibly fed. They had many slogans and mottos, one of which was 'make more noise'.

ROSA MAY BILLINGHURST (1875–1953)
Imprisoned and force-fed, she was often seen in her three-wheeled wheelchair at suffragette protests, and went on raids to drop ink bombs into postboxes around London.

EMMELINE PETHICK-LAWRENCE (1867–1954)
Treasurer of the WSPU and co-editor of *Votes For Women*, she created the green, white and purple colour scheme of the WSPU. She was both imprisoned and force-fed.

FREDERICK PETHICK-LAWRENCE (1871–1961)
The only man to help with the management of the WSPU, he was the husband of Emmeline. He became an MP in 1923, beating his old enemy, Winston Churchill, in the election.

'GENERAL' FLORA DRUMMOND (1879–1949)
A key organizer for the WSPU's Scottish branch, she later moved to London. She got her nickname by often riding her horse at the front of processions, dressed in a military-style uniform.

JULIA SCURR (1871–1927)

A member of the East London Federation of Suffragettes (ELFS), in 1914 she led a delegation to the Prime Minister protesting about women's low wages.

EMILY WILDING DAVISON (1872–1913)

Fiercely militant, she was frequently imprisoned and force-fed. Once she barricaded herself into her cell, and the guards filled it with water from a hose, before the door was broken down.

MARY LEIGH (1885–1978)

One of the first window smashers, she was involved in many of the most eye-catching suffragette protests. Frequently imprisoned and force-fed, she was also a drum major in the WSPU band.

UNA DUGDALE (1880–1978)

She caused a scandal by wanting to cut 'obey' from her wedding vows, although she did not, when told it would invalidate her marriage. She later wrote a pamphlet entitled *Love and Honour But Not Obey*.

EDITH NEW (1877–1951)

A schoolteacher and militant campaigner for the WSPU, she was one of the first window smashers and was imprisoned – and force-fed – many times.

EDITH GARRUD (1872–1971)

A ju-jitsu instructor, she trained the suffragettes in self-defence, in particular the bodyguard of thirty women known as the 'Amazons' whose job it was to protect the leaders of the WSPU.

PRINCESS SOPHIA DULEEP SINGH (1876–1948)

A member of the Tax Resistance League and the WSPU, the authorities refused to send her to prison because of her royal connections. She went on to become a nurse in the First World War.

CHRISTABEL PANKHURST (1880–1958)

Emmeline Pankhurst's eldest daughter became the key strategist for the WSPU, and was one of its most powerful public speakers with a high profile in the national press.

LADY CONSTANCE LYTTON (1869–1923)

She exposed the double standards of treatment for working-class and upper-class prisoners by dressing as a seamstress and going by the name of Jane Wharton, in which disguise she was force-fed.

Suffragist

Democratic

Run like a union

NUWSS and all other suffrage societies

Leaders chosen by members

Peaceful and law-abiding

No slogan

Believed that the violent acts committed by the suffragettes damaged the cause of women's suffrage and hindered support

Included men as members of male suffrage societies and supporters of women's suffrage

Continued throughout the war to protest for women's votes

Maintained peaceful protest throughout the whole campaign

 Campaigning began in mid-1800s

Suffragette

Autocratic

Run like an army

WSPU

Leaders
not elected

Militant, law-breaking,
ready to commit
civil disobedience

'Deeds Not Words'

Believed that violent acts
(only ever committed
against property, not
human life) would be
the only way to force
change

Did not really want to
have men as members,
since women should
be independent

Ceased all
militant action on
the declaration of
war in 1914

 Campaigning
began in 1903

 Acts of civil
disobedience from
1905 to 1914

1907: Mud, Mud, Mud!

THE WEATHER ON SATURDAY, 9 FEBRUARY 1907 WAS DREADFUL: POURING RAIN, FREEZING COLD AND FOGGY. THE STREETS OF LONDON WERE HEAVY WITH WET, SPLATTERING MUD.

This was not a day you would expect to find ladies in fine dresses and elegant hats marching through the streets carrying banners proclaiming 'Failure Is Impossible', 'Be Right and Persist' and 'Justice Not Privilege'. But that is the spectacle that thousands of onlookers witnessed that day in London.

It was the first big procession organized by the NUWSS to show the government and the public that, contrary to what they thought, lots of women *did* want the vote.

The Artists' Suffrage League designed posters and postcards advertising the event. Women 'of all classes' were urged to 'take part in this procession and prove your earnestness in a manner both effective and constitutional'.

This was to be a dignified, law-abiding procession. Participants were to assemble at the Band Stand at Hyde Park Corner at 2 p.m. and parade to Exeter Hall in the Strand, where various speakers would address a campaign meeting.

More than 3,000 women from over forty suffrage societies turned up in the rain to walk the two-mile route.

Millicent Fawcett, who had helped to arrange the march, remarked, 'The London weather did its worst against us. Mud, mud, mud was its prominent feature.'

But this did not deter the women who came from all over the country and from every class and profession: factory workers, textile workers and nurses marched alongside artists, writers and doctors. Posh ladies from rich and famous families and ordinary working-class women all came together that day.

The WSPU had not been officially invited because some of the other societies like the Women's Liberal Federation (WLF) and the British Women's Temperance Association (BWTA) did not approve of their militant actions, but some came anyway, and a small group of suffragettes sneaked in to march alongside the others.

What a spectacle it must have been, with the hats, ribbons and scarves in the NUWSS colours of red and white blowing in the wind amid all that rain and mud.

We are quite used to seeing people marching to protest against government decisions nowadays, but back in 1907 it would have been unusual and even quite shocking to see so many women join a protest march. The press loved it, and filled their newspapers with reports from the day.

These women were incredibly brave. Some of them worried they might ruin their reputations by being seen in public this way, while others were afraid they might lose their jobs. But they were bringing attention to their cause, which they considered worth the risk.

What became known as the 'Mud March' was considered a tremendous success. Many, many more marches would follow, showing the government and those opposed to women's suffrage that women would stand together, shoulder to shoulder, friend to friend, in their struggle to win the vote.

1907: 'Dare to Be Free'

FRIENDS SOMETIMES FALL OUT WITH EACH OTHER, ESPECIALLY IF THEY WON'T LISTEN TO EACH OTHER'S POINT OF VIEW.

Christabel and Emmeline Pankurst were both extremely strict leaders; they, together with Emmeline Pethick-Lawrence, made all the major decisions regarding the WSPU. Most members were happy with that arrangement, but any who disagreed with them had no choice but to put up with it or leave.

In 1907, a small group of Christabel and Emmeline's friends challenged them to make the WSPU more democratic. Their answer was a resounding, 'NO!', and so Charlotte Despard, along with seventy other women, broke free from the WSPU to form the Women's Freedom League (WFL).

The WFL's members were mostly pacifists, which meant they were against war or violence of any kind.

Unlike the WSPU, which like the NUWSS was focused mainly on winning the vote for women on the same terms as men (which meant the wealthier, middle-class women), the WFL declared they wanted votes for *all* men and women, on equal terms, rich and poor. Like the WSPU, they also wanted to see women get equal pay with men, and to receive equal job opportunities. With their motto, 'Dare to Be Free', they very soon had thousands of enthusiastic members.

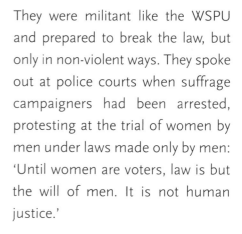

The WFL worked hard. They printed their own newspaper called *The Vote*, which was very well written and became a great way for them to criticize the government.

To gain new recruits, they travelled the country in a horse-drawn caravan, stopping off in towns and villages to give speeches and to sell the newspaper.

They were militant like the WSPU and prepared to break the law, but only in non-violent ways. They spoke out at police courts when suffrage campaigners had been arrested, protesting at the trial of women by men under laws made only by men: 'Until women are voters, law is but the will of men. It is not human justice.'

They even visited members of the government at home in order to put their case, and in 1909 members of the WFL protested peacefully outside the House of Commons for three months, demanding to speak directly to the Prime Minister, who ignored them.

One hundred WFL members were sent to prison because one of their main weapons of protest was to refuse to pay tax. Their argument was the same as Mary Smith's had been when she wrote her petition in 1832: why should women pay tax to a government over which, without a vote, they had no influence at all? Their campaign of 'No taxation without representation' was a practical and effective tool against government.

1907: Votes for Women? Never!

'THE CAT, THE WOMAN AND THE CHIMNEY SHOULD NEVER LEAVE THE HOUSE.' THIS OLD SAYING, SHOCKING TO OUR EARS, SUMS UP HOW MANY PEOPLE IN BRITAIN STILL FELT AT THE TURN OF THE TWENTIETH CENTURY.

The very thought of giving women the parliamentary vote was exceedingly unpopular – among both men and women. Women were seen by many as physically, emotionally, intellectually inferior to men. How could they possibly be trusted to cast a vote?

As the suffragist campaign grew and spoke with a louder, stronger voice, the people who were opposed to women voting spoke up too. They became known as the National League for Opposing Women's Suffrage, or the 'Antis', and they all had a jolly good laugh at the men and women who were campaigning for change. Some people don't like change, it makes them nervous, and the Antis were very nervous about what the country, even the world, would look like if women were making important political decisions.

The Antis made all sorts of extraordinary claims as to why women should not be allowed to vote: a woman was ruled by impulse and emotion, and could never think logically; a woman's mind was full of what society considered to be childish thoughts, like what hat to wear, or what pretty dress to buy, which dreamy man

to marry, gossip, chocolate, babies, puppies and kittens. They said women were irrational, fickle and unable to make reasonable judgements. They should stay at home, sewing, doing embroidery and drinking tea. One MP remarked, 'Votes for women? What shall we be asked next? To give votes to our horses and dogs?'

Advertisements were placed in newspapers and magazines, and postcards and posters were printed, all designed to undermine the campaign for votes for women. Some even made fun of protesting women with the childish prank of pinning insulting labels on their backs.

But you would be wrong to presume that these ideas came only from men, exerting their assumed superiority over women. Some of the most outspoken opponents to women's suffrage were women themselves, who said they were perfectly happy to let their menfolk make decisions on their behalf, and believed that if they gained the vote on equal terms with men, it would bring about an end to family life, even an end to civilization itself. At a time when the likelihood of war seemed very present, there was also a real fear, among both men and women, that if women voted, the country would embrace pacifism, resulting in men refusing to fight in a war to defend the country.

In any case, it was believed by many that most women didn't even want the vote.

Notable Antis

THE NATIONAL LEAGUE FOR OPPOSING WOMEN'S SUFFRAGE WAS FORMED WHEN THE WOMEN'S NATIONAL ANTI-SUFFRAGE LEAGUE JOINED WITH THE MEN'S LEAGUE FOR OPPOSING WOMAN SUFFRAGE IN 1910.

At its peak in 1914, the membership reached 42,000, only one in five of which were men. It is surprising that so many women were opposed to their own enfranchisement, but they clearly felt they had the support of the public when over 300,000 people signed a petition against votes for women.

Some of the strongest Antis were also social reformers and keen campaigners for improving the education and living standards for the poor, especially for women. And yet they held an unflinching belief that women should be kept well away from the complexities of politics.

While many remained firmly against women's suffrage, some changed their minds in time, and went on to support it.

GERTRUDE BELL (1868–1926)
An archaeologist and explorer, she travelled all over the world, and even established the Iraq Museum in Baghdad, an extraordinary achievement. Strangely, she was also one of the leaders of the Anti-Suffrage League, believing that most women lacked the education needed to understand politics, so that a vote would be wasted on them.

LORD CURZON (1859–1925)
Viceroy of India and later Foreign Secretary, he was an opponent of women's suffrage and in 1910 appealed for support in the *Times* newspaper. One man replied, 'More men than you perhaps guess have nothing but pity left for the rubbish you talk.' Undaunted, Lord Curzon became president of the National League for Opposing Woman Suffrage in 1912.

QUEEN VICTORIA (1819–1901)
During her sixty-three-year reign (1837–1901), she was one of the most powerful leaders in the world, yet remained fiercely opposed to 'Women's Rights', which she once called 'a wicked folly'. One of her daughters, Princess Louise, met with suffragists in private, but could not offer support in public because of her mother's views.

ETHEL BERTHA HARRISON (1851–1916)
A wealthy society lady, educated by both French and English governesses both in London and France, she was one of the leaders of the Women's National Anti-Suffrage League, and wrote anti-suffrage essays, expressing her opinion that women were by nature unsuited to political activities. She also wrote and published a series of hymns.

MRS HUMPHRY WARD (1851–1920)
Using her married name, she was a successful novelist and a founder of the Women's Anti-Suffrage League. On her death, the writer Virginia Woolf (a supporter of women's suffrage) said scathingly, 'Mrs Ward is dead; poor Mrs Humphry Ward; and it appears that she was merely a woman of straw after all – shovelled into the ground and already forgotten.'

LADY JERSEY (1849–1945)
Lady Jersey was one of several members of the aristocracy involved in the formation of the Women's National Anti-Suffrage League and chaired their first meeting, held on 21 July 1908 at the Westminster Palace Hotel in London. She believed that to give women the vote in parliamentary elections would prove little short of a disaster.

HERBERT HENRY (HH) ASQUITH (1852–1928)
As Prime Minister from 1908 to 1916, the suffragettes considered him their most bitter enemy. He dashed their hopes whenever it looked as if a law might be passed to give women the vote. At the same time, he did introduce radical laws to provide pensions for the elderly and financial support for the unemployed, disabled and ill.

WINSTON CHURCHILL (1874–1965)
As Home Secretary, he was responsible for repressing the militant activism of the suffragettes, who blamed him for the atrocities of 'Black Friday'. He claimed women did not need the vote because they were 'well represented by their fathers, brothers and husbands', but later changed his mind and voted in favour of limited women's suffrage in 1918.

VIOLET MARKHAM (1872–1959)
She worked to improve the lives of the poor and the unemployed all her life, but was also a keen supporter of the Women's Anti-Suffrage League. Having campaigned hard against women getting the vote, speaking out at major venues including the Albert Hall in London, she herself stood for Parliament in the general election of 1918. She lost, but later became Mayor of Chesterfield.

THE DUCHESS OF MONTROSE (1854–1940)
President of the Scottish National Anti-Suffrage League, she believed woman were incapable of making political decisions. And yet she used her own wealth and position in society to support many good causes, from the training of midwives and nurses, to holiday homes for children in poverty. She was also president of the Scottish Red Cross.

1908: Breaking Glass

THE SUFFRAGETTES' MOTTO OF 'DEEDS, NOT WORDS' WAS WORKING, AND ACTS OF CIVIL DISOBEDIENCE BY MEMBERS OF THE WSPU WERE BECOMING MUCH MORE COMMON.

Now the sound of women heckling politicians was joined by a new sound that reached the very heart of the government: the sound of breaking glass. It would prove to be a very powerful noise indeed.

On 30 June 1908, two suffragettes, Mary Leigh and Edith New, went to Downing Street armed with stones. When they arrived at Number 10, they flung the stones at the windows, smashing and shattering the glass. Of course, they were both arrested, and were sent to Holloway Prison for two months.

This wasn't their first act of civil disobedience. Edith had previously been arrested for chaining herself to the railings at 10 Downing Street, and Mary had been sent to prison in 1907 when a suffragette march to Parliament turned violent.

It was, however, seen as the first act of vandalism by suffragettes. Over the coming years, hundreds of windows would be smashed, causing thousands of pounds' worth of damage, in the fight to win the vote.

On their release from jail, Mary and Edith were treated as heroines by their fellow suffragettes, who met them at the prison gates and took them to a celebratory breakfast held in their honour. They travelled in an open carriage drawn not by horses, but by a team of suffragettes, accompanied by rousing brass bands.

Rather than apologize for their violent actions, they made the government this threat: if women don't get the vote, 'It will be bombs next time!'

1908: Prime Enemy

THE SUFFRAGETTES KNEW THEY WERE FIGHTING A WAR. THEY HAD MANY ENEMIES, BUT PERHAPS THEIR MOST BOTHERSOME, UNYIELDING FOE WAS THE PRIME MINISTER HIMSELF.

Herbert Henry Asquith, known as 'HH' for short, became the leader of the Liberal Party and Prime Minister of the UK in April 1908. This was not good news for the suffragettes: HH was firmly set against giving women the vote. Many Liberal MPs did support votes for women, but Mr Asquith just didn't take the idea of women voters seriously. He refused to believe that the public supported women's suffrage and demanded proof that society would be better if women had the vote, or indeed that most women even wanted the vote.

The suffragists answered him by holding a huge rally in London's Hyde Park in 1908 with well over 250,000 – some say even half a million – people, all chanting, 'Votes for women!'

But still he would not listen, and repeatedly declined to meet with leaders of the various women's suffrage societies, in particular the WSPU.

The suffragettes were getting on his nerves. He was their main target, and they attacked him whenever they could get close enough. He was jeered at, slapped and even whipped. On one occasion, a pleasant game of golf in Scotland was ruined when two suffragettes got on to the course and began to harangue him. (Mr Asquith was particularly vexed about that.)

They jumped on his car, smashed his windows, and chained themselves to his railings. In Birmingham, they threw roof slates at him. In Dublin, they tried to burn down the theatre where he was due to give a speech, and on the same visit to Ireland, Mary Leigh even hurled an axe at the carriage in which he was travelling. Luckily it missed, but it did cut the ear of the MP he was with, John Redmond.

All this did nothing to change the Prime Minister's mind. In fact, it only made him more stubborn.

Eventually he did agree to meet with the more peaceful, non-axe-wielding Millicent Fawcett and a small group from the NUWSS. But no matter what they said, he wouldn't budge. Over the years of his Prime Ministership, he remained steadfastly opposed to women voters, and so the war between the suffragettes and the Prime Minister raged on.

1908: The 'Trojan Horse Raid'

SUFFRAGETTES WERE FREQUENTLY STOPPED FROM ENTERING PARLIAMENT BUILDINGS. HECKLING, BOOING, EVEN PHYSICAL ATTACKS ON MPS HAD WORN THE PATIENCE OF THE GOVERNMENT PAPER-THIN.

The government was so nervous that Parliament was on occasion surrounded by an army of policemen to stop the women from getting in.

But suffragettes didn't give up so easily, especially Christabel Pankhurst, who thought up a new tactic. When a big furniture van trundled up to the gates one day in 1908, the police thought nothing of it, parted ranks, and let the van pass through.

No sooner was it inside than over twenty suffragettes leaped from the back and made a dash for the entrance to the building. The startled police gave chase and grabbed all but two, who barged straight into Parliament shouting, 'Votes for women!'

The newspapers thought this was hilarious, and called it the 'Trojan Horse Raid'. The story of how the suffragettes outwitted the police was reported as far away as New Zealand, where the *Auckland Star* commented, 'Such determination and pluck must surely win in the end.'

There was still a long way to go, but through such exploits the campaign for votes for women was getting noticed.

The Rebel Princess

SOPHIA DULEEP SINGH WAS A SUFFRAGETTE, A POLITICAL REBEL AND . . . A PRINCESS.

Her grandfather was the Great Maharaja Ranjit Singh, who was so powerful he was nicknamed 'The Lion of the Punjab'. But when he died, his son, Duleep Singh, Sophia's father, was only a child, and the British, who at the time ruled India, forced him to sign away all his inheritance.

Duleep was exiled from India to England at the age of fifteen, where he became a favourite of Queen Victoria. When his daughter, Princess Sophia, was born in 1876, Queen Victoria became her godmother.

Princess Sophia grew up in high society, mingling with aristocrats and royalty. As a child, she had cheetahs and leopards as pets, and as she grew up, her face was in all the magazines, just like a celebrity of today.

But Princess Sophia was troubled by how her family had been cheated by the British, and came to realize she needed more than fancy clothes and parties to fill her life.

Then in 1908 she met Una Dugdale, a suffragette who told Sophia exciting stories about the WSPU. Sophia's imagination was caught and she decided to dedicate herself to the fight for women's rights.

Sophia would regularly sell the newspaper *The Suffragette* outside her home: Hampton Court Palace. It was brilliant publicity for the campaign. She also joined the Women's Tax Resistance League, who refused to pay any tax until women were given the right to vote: 'No vote, no tax.'

The government knew how embarrassing it would be for them to arrest a princess, and especially one so well known and popular with the public, so they tried to ignore Sophia. But in the end they had no choice but to fine her for her unpaid tax. Bailiffs were sent to Hampton Court Palace to remove her jewellery so it could be sold at auction to pay her debt.

Then something extraordinary happened. Each time Sophia's jewellery was to be sold, the auction house would fill with rich ladies, but no one would bid. Instead of the price going up, it would go down, right down, until just one lady would bid, buying the jewellery for a pittance. Next, in a show of sheer defiance to the authorities, whoever had bought the jewellery would make a big display of handing it back to Princess Sophia, who always just happened to be in the audience.

The suffragettes were still finding new ways to defy the government and bring attention to their campaign.

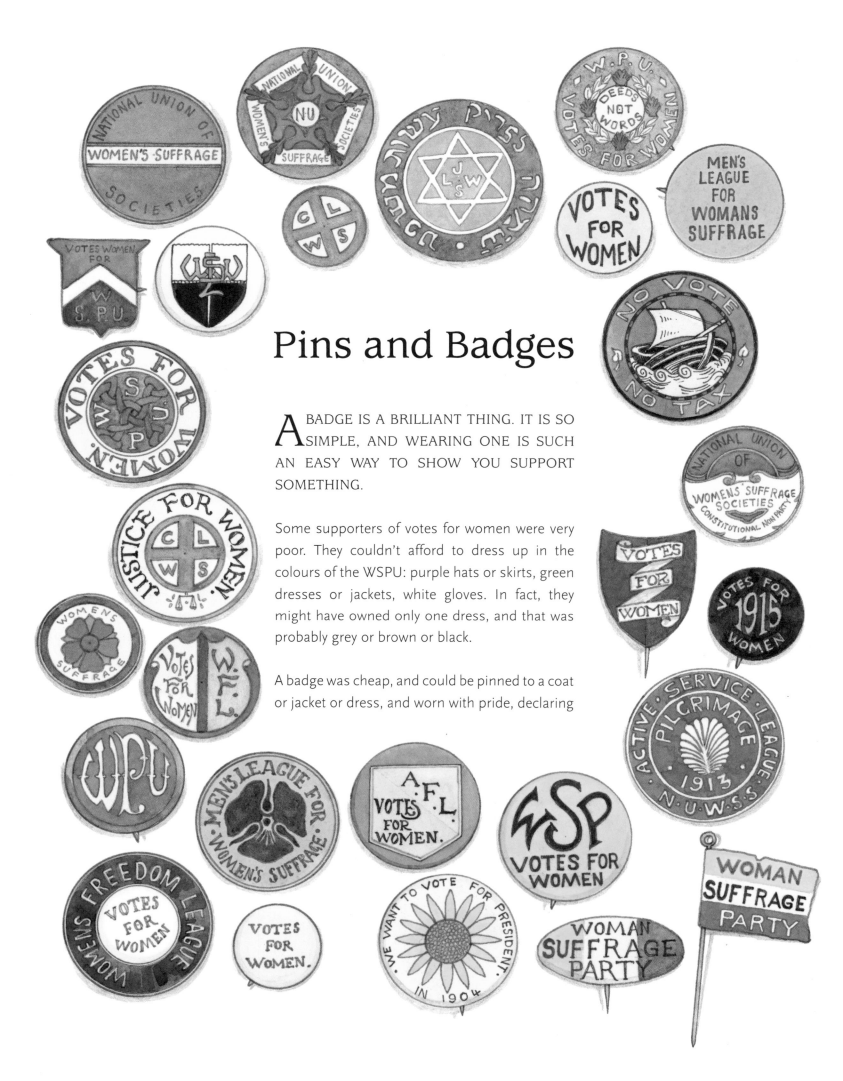

Pins and Badges

A BADGE IS A BRILLIANT THING. IT IS SO SIMPLE, AND WEARING ONE IS SUCH AN EASY WAY TO SHOW YOU SUPPORT SOMETHING.

Some supporters of votes for women were very poor. They couldn't afford to dress up in the colours of the WSPU: purple hats or skirts, green dresses or jackets, white gloves. In fact, they might have owned only one dress, and that was probably grey or brown or black.

A badge was cheap, and could be pinned to a coat or jacket or dress, and worn with pride, declaring to everyone that its wearer was a supporter of votes for women. Lots of suffrage groups made badges, usually in the colours of each group.

Badges were popular both in the UK and America, like the ones on the page opposite from the Women's Freedom League, the Men's League for Women's Suffrage, the NUWSS, the Women's Political Union, the Church League for Women's Suffrage, the Women Writers' Suffrage League, the WSPU, the Jewish League for Women's Suffrage, the Women's Tax Resistance League, the Actresses' Franchise League and the Women's Suffrage Party.

Of course, the Antis had badges too. The Women's National Anti-Suffrage League and the National League for Opposing Woman Suffrage both decorated their badges with a rose, a thistle and a clover, representing England, Scotland and Ireland, as a united force saying a very firm 'NO' to votes for women.

1909: Hunger Strike

PRISON IN BRITAIN IN THE EARLY TWENTIETH CENTURY WAS HORRIBLE; MUCH WORSE THAN IT IS TODAY. DRAUGHTY AND COLD IN WINTER; HOT AND MUGGY IN SUMMER; STINKY ALL YEAR ROUND; HARD PRISON BEDS, NO MORE THAN PLANKS OF WOOD, TO SLEEP ON; ICE-COLD WATER TO WASH IN; DIMLY LIT AND GRIM: PRISON WAS A PLACE TO BE AVOIDED AT ALL COSTS.

So even if you disagree with the law-breaking antics of the militant suffragettes, it is hard not to acknowledge the incredible bravery and courage it took for them to knowingly break the law, understanding as they did that they would be sent to jail.

Most judges offered them a choice of a fine or a prison sentence, but most suffragettes chose prison.

Of course this scandalized and shocked the public. But the suffragettes recognized its value in attracting attention and sympathy for their cause, especially the sight of refined, educated, respectable ladies being treated so brutally by the authorities.

At the time, prisoners were separated into three divisions. The third division was for ordinary criminals, whose sentences were often accompanied by 'hard labour', meaning they were given tough physical tasks to perform as part of their punishment.

The second division was for prisoners considered to be of better character, or who were being imprisoned for more minor offences such as refusing to pay a fine. These prisoners had to spend the first four weeks of their sentence in solitary confinement, unable to speak to anyone. During their time in prison they were allowed no books, and almost no visitors. They were not even allowed to send or receive letters and so had no news from home or about what was happening in the outside world.

Meanwhile first-division prisoners had newspapers as well as books, and were allowed to correspond with their friends and family as well as have frequent visits from them. They wore their own clothes and were even allowed to send out for their own food. Political prisoners were classed as first division.

On entering prison, the suffragettes always demanded to be allowed this special treatment given to political prisoners – after all, they were fighting the government on a political point. But the authorities were having none of that. They treated the suffragettes just the same as any ordinary criminal, usually as second-division, but sometimes even as third-division prisoners.

The suffragettes had to wear prison uniform: white cap, rough black dress covered in white arrows, white cotton apron covered with black arrows, itchy red-and-brown-striped stockings, and tatty old shoes that were probably full of holes. Big round leather labels were pinned to their clothes, printed with their cell numbers.

No letters or visitors; no books or newspapers. There was only hard work, and horrid, bland prison food.

In 1909, at Holloway Prison in London, one prisoner had an idea about how she could carry on her protest to win votes for women while still being locked up. She went on hunger strike.

The prisoner's name was Marion Wallace-Dunlop. She was an artist, serving a month-long prison sentence for graffiti in the House of Commons where she had printed a

protest message on a wall with a rubber stamp.

Three days into her sentence, Marion refused to eat anything. For several days the prison authorities tried to tempt her to eat by replacing the normal poor, boring prison food with delicious meals that would be left all day long in her cell to torment her. But Marion wouldn't eat a crumb.

There was a real fear that she might starve herself to death, so after ninety-one hours on hunger strike, Marion was released from prison.

Hunger strike was no fun at all. The pain and misery of hunger would cause depression, stomach pain, headache, dizziness and exhaustion. But Marion had started something that would inspire hundreds more suffragette prisoners to do the same.

It caused consternation for the prison authorities. They didn't know what to do, except to release the hunger strikers from their prison sentences early, when they became so weak it looked as if they might actually die. They were losing control of the situation.

But it didn't take long before a royal voice spoke up, with a menacing suggestion. The King himself wondered why on earth these women were not being forcibly fed.

1909: The Gag, the Tube and the Funnel

TO BE FORCE-FED WAS TORTURE, A HORROR SUFFRAGETTES LIKE ELSIE DUVAL AND HUGH FRANKLIN KNEW ONLY TOO WELL.

The prisoner was held, or even tied, to a bed or chair by the prison wardens. Then a painful metal gag would be pushed into the prisoner's mouth to prise it open, and a rubber tube forced down their throat. If that failed, the tube was shoved up their nose instead. Then a sloppy gloop of eggy, milky, bready goo was poured through a funnel down the tube, directly into their stomach.

Hundreds of suffragettes and their supporters, both women and men, were force-fed. They described the unbearable pain in the nose and throat and chest, the pounding in the head and heart that felt like being choked. Sometimes in the struggle the sloppy gloop would end up in the prisoner's lungs, leaving them gravely ill. Often they just sicked the whole lot back up anyway.

One famous case was that of Lady Constance Lytton. She was arrested during a WSPU protest at the House of Commons, sent to prison, and went on hunger strike. But unlike working-class prisoners, she was seen by a doctor and released early, without being forcibly fed. Lady Constance became suspicious that she was being treated differently because of who she was. So she cut her hair, put on a shabby dress and disguised herself as a poor seamstress.

In this disguise, she was arrested while protesting in Liverpool, sent to prison, and again went on hunger strike. This time, because the authorities thought she was a 'nobody', no doctor checked her health, and she was forcibly fed. Eventually her real identity was discovered, upon which she was immediately released, but she never quite recovered from the ordeal, and some historians believe it contributed to her early death.

Force-feeding of suffragette prisoners soon became very unpopular with the public. Many MPs were disgusted that the government had agreed to it, one calling it a 'beastly outrage', and 116 doctors signed a petition against it. The government didn't know what to do. Some options discussed in Parliament at the time included carting the hunger strikers off to lunatic asylums, shipping them off overseas, or even just letting them die.

Giving women the vote was also mentioned, but only as a joke: the government were not about to do that. So they did nothing, and the hunger strikes – and the force-feeding continued.

1909: The Magnificent Muriel Matters in her Flying Machine

MURIEL MATTERS WAS TRULY MAGNIFICENT. AN ACTOR, MUSICIAN AND LATER A VERY TALENTED JOURNALIST, SHE FOUND IMAGINATIVE WAYS TO GRAB ATTENTION TO THE CAUSE OF VOTES FOR WOMEN.

Muriel was an Australian who moved to the UK in 1905. Two years later, she became a member of the Women's Freedom League (WFL), who believed in action and protest, but only in a non-violent way.

In October 1908, Muriel chained herself to a metal grille in the Ladies' Gallery at the House of Commons, in protest at the grille being there to separate women from men, since in fact it obstructed their view of Parliament below. She attached herself so well, the whole grille had to be removed, with Muriel still attached to it, while a blacksmith was sent for to cut her free.

But her most daring deed came a year later.

Her friend Henry Spencer had built an 80-foot hydrogen-filled airship, which gave Muriel an idea. On 16 February 1909, King Edward VII was due to lead a procession for the State Opening of Parliament. What if an airship were to fly overhead, raining down 'Votes for Women' leaflets on the King, the procession, the Houses of Parliament, and the crowds below?

The airship was painted on one side with 'Votes for Women' and on the other with 'The Women's Freedom League', all in huge letters so the words could be read for miles around. On the day, the basket was loaded up with leaflets, and the intrepid Muriel climbed in, followed by Henry. Up, up, up they rose, to a height of 3,500 feet.

It was extremely cold up there in the sky high above London, but to keep warm Muriel busied herself throwing out leaflets. She watched nervously as Henry climbed out of the basket and clambered across the delicate frame to make adjustments to the rigging. He made her think of a spider creeping across its web. Suddenly she realized that if Henry fell off, she had no idea how to fly the airship. But she tried not to think about that, and carried on 'making a trail of leaflets across London'.

Unfortunately, it was a blustery day, so the airship was blown off course and never made it to the sky above the King's procession. Nonetheless, Muriel flew over the outskirts of London for over an hour, dropping leaflets on to the streets below . . . before crash-landing into a tree at Coulsdon in Surrey.

Despite things not going entirely to plan, the flight was declared a great success, and the story of the valiant Muriel Matters and her airship featured in newspapers around the world.

Pageants and Parades

THE SUFFRAGISTS AND SUFFRAGETTES KNEW HOW TO PUT ON A GOOD SHOW.

All those years spent learning 'women's work' came in very handy indeed. Crafts that women had been doing since they were little girls were put to great use as they embroidered banners and flags, painted posters, designed badges and jewellery, and knitted scarves.

They wrote poems, performed plays and organized spectacular parades, all with the intention of showing the public and the government the importance of women's achievements, past and present.

They also loved dressing up, particularly as great women from history. The fifteenth-century French heroine Joan of Arc on horseback was a favourite, representing female rebellion. Others dressed as the novelist Charlotte Brontë, Queen Boadicea or Queen Elizabeth I, representing wisdom, strength and power respectively.

Different groups of women would march together. For example, some parades were held to celebrate women at work, featuring such professions as nurses, midwives, actresses, journalists and teachers. Or else women from England, Ireland, Scotland and Wales might join forces and march in their thousands, often wearing traditional or national dress, while Indian women would parade together wearing saris.

Women who had been to jail wanted everyone to know, and would make replica costumes of prison uniforms covered in arrows, or proudly carry a pole with an arrow at the top.

The atmosphere was always jubilant. Marching bands would play cheery songs and the women would sing along. In fact the songs were so catchy that the crowds of spectators would often join in too.

These pageants and parades were a real spectacle, all designed to draw attention to the cause of votes for women.

But was the government listening?

1909: The Bingley Hall Brouhaha

ONE GOOD WAY FOR THE SUFFRAGETTES TO GET PUBLICITY FOR THEIR CAUSE WAS TO HECKLE POLITICIANS WHEN THEY WERE SPEAKING IN PUBLIC.

Their disruptive, 'unladylike' behaviour got them banned from attending political meetings, so the suffragettes thought up unusual, inventive and sometimes startling methods to continue this form of protest. They hid in buildings where political meetings were due to take place, tucked behind organ pipes or crouched beneath platforms, often for hours on end, ready to leap out when the meeting was in full flow.

They were sometimes even lowered down into meetings on ropes from the skylights. Or they climbed up on to the rooftops of buildings near political venues to hurl missiles through the windows where a meeting was in progress.

The Prime Minister, Herbert Henry Asquith, was an obvious target and was harassed by the suffragettes on numerous occasions. On 17 September 1909, Asquith was giving a speech at Bingley Hall in Birmingham. No women were allowed into the building, which was surrounded by police.

Mary Leigh and eight other suffragettes climbed up on to the roof of the building opposite, armed with axes. They proceeded to hack slates off the roof and hurl them down at the police below. The police returned the attack, and pelted them with bricks and stones, then turned a hose on the women clinging to the roof, who demanded to speak to the Prime Minister. Eventually three policemen managed to climb up and arrest them.

Mary was sent to prison for four months with hard labour, which meant she was made to do exhausting physical work during her sentence.

On arriving at prison, she broke a window in protest, demanding that she be treated as a political prisoner. When she was refused, Mary followed the example of Marion Wallace-Dunlop and went on hunger strike. She was one of the first suffragettes to be forcibly fed.

This was not Mary's first time in prison. During 1908 as a result of her protests, she had spent a total of more than six months in jail. A passionate suffragette, she remained undeterred, continuing her activities even when she was released from prison after being forcibly fed. Her protests took many forms: Mary Leigh was also a drum major in the WSPU's drum and fife band, which often played at their marches and processions.

A Riot of Colour

LOOKING AT PHOTOGRAPHS OF SUFFRAGISTS ON MARCHES AND CAMPAIGNS, WE SEE A WORLD IN BLACK AND WHITE, BUT IN REALITY IT WOULD HAVE BEEN A RIOT OF COLOUR.

All the women's suffrage organizations had banners and flags in their own particular colour scheme. Sometimes the colours had meanings.

The most famous colour scheme was the green, purple and white of the WSPU. People sometimes refer to the colour purple as violet, which created a myth about the meaning behind these three colours. It was said that if you take the 'G' from green, the 'W' from white, and the 'V' from violet, you have GWV – a code that meant 'Give Women Votes'. This isn't true, but it is a nice idea.

But the colours do have meanings: Green represents 'Hope', White 'Purity', and Purple/Violet represents 'Dignity'. These colours were first used in 1908 when they were chosen by Emmeline Pethick-Lawrence.

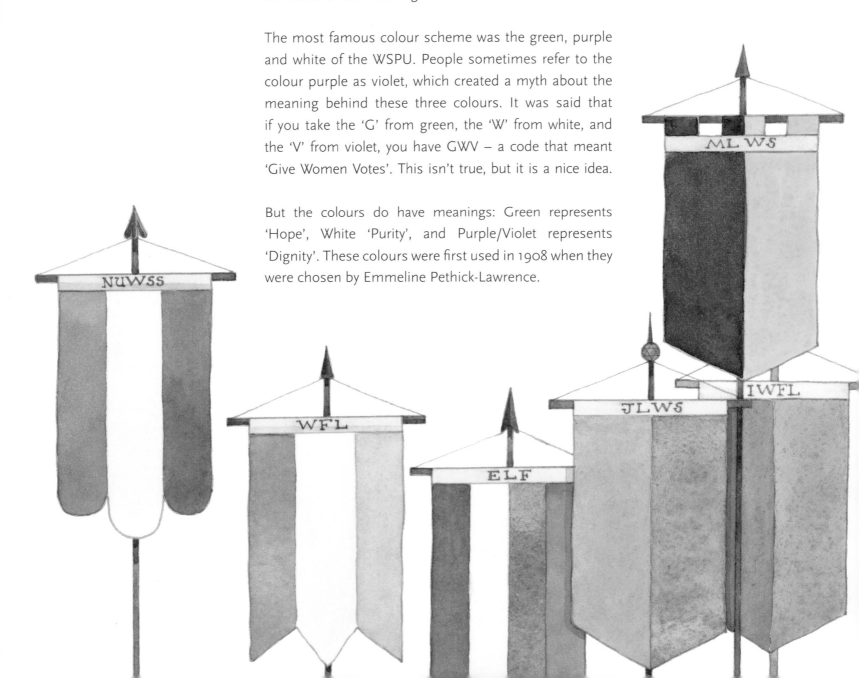

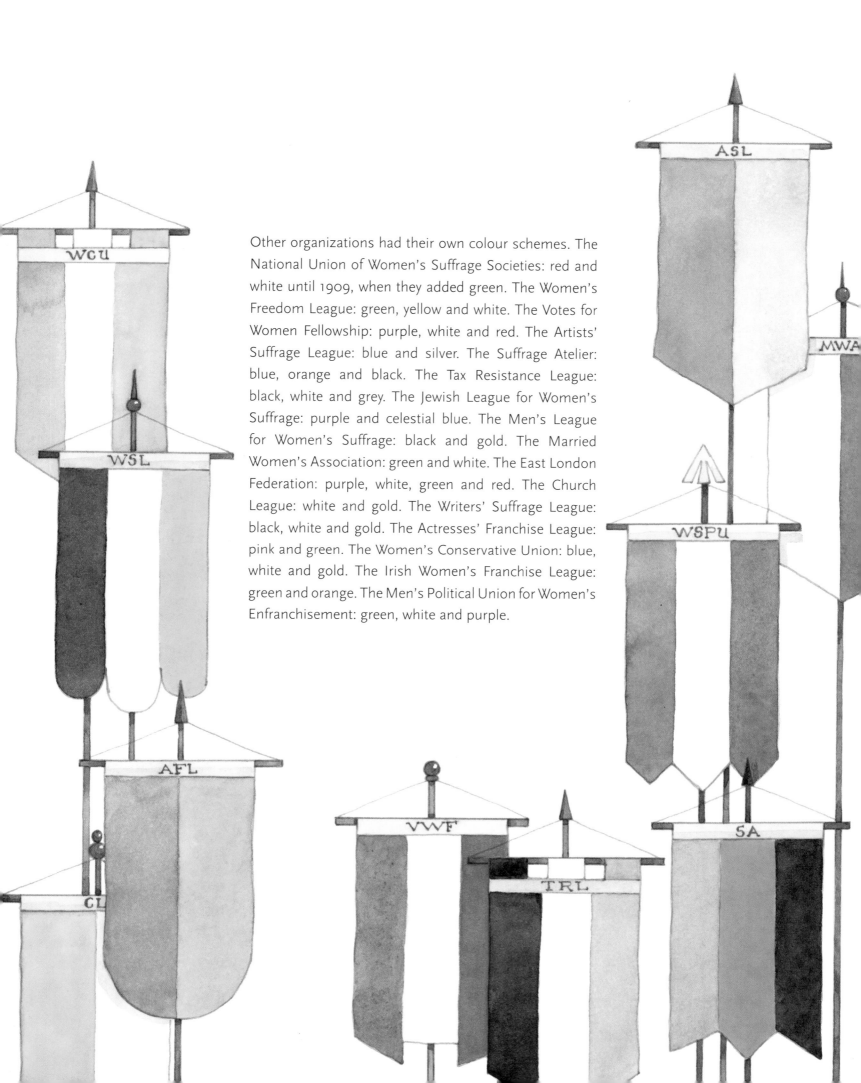

Other organizations had their own colour schemes. The National Union of Women's Suffrage Societies: red and white until 1909, when they added green. The Women's Freedom League: green, yellow and white. The Votes for Women Fellowship: purple, white and red. The Artists' Suffrage League: blue and silver. The Suffrage Atelier: blue, orange and black. The Tax Resistance League: black, white and grey. The Jewish League for Women's Suffrage: purple and celestial blue. The Men's League for Women's Suffrage: black and gold. The Married Women's Association: green and white. The East London Federation: purple, white, green and red. The Church League: white and gold. The Writers' Suffrage League: black, white and gold. The Actresses' Franchise League: pink and green. The Women's Conservative Union: blue, white and gold. The Irish Women's Franchise League: green and orange. The Men's Political Union for Women's Enfranchisement: green, white and purple.

1910–1912: The Bill, the Whole Bill and Nothing but the Bill

A 'BILL' DESIGNED TO GIVE WOMEN THE VOTE WAS WRITTEN AND READ IN PARLIAMENT EVERY YEAR FROM 1900.

A bill is when an idea for a new law, or a change to an existing law, is written down to be read and discussed by MPs in Parliament. MPs can then decide if they like the idea or not, and so vote for (or against) the bill to create (or prevent) an 'Act of Parliament' that will bring about a new law.

At first Parliament didn't take the idea of giving women the vote seriously at all, and any bill on the subject would be laughed at, abandoned, or 'talked out', which meant that MPs just kept talking about any other topic (for example, in 1904, on the effectiveness of tail lights on what was then a brand-new invention: the motor car). The idea was to keep talking until the time ran out and they all went home, having not even discussed women's votes, let alone having passed the bill to make it law.

The suffragists and suffragettes were exasperated each time their bill was dropped, ignored or rejected. By 1908 most MPs did support giving women the vote, although they could not agree on exactly *which* women: only those who owned property, or a wider group including working-class women?

In 1910 something called a Conciliation Bill was written. The idea was to find a compromise on the subject of women's votes, to 'conciliate' or pacify those who thought it an important issue. Instead of asking for the law to change to allow all women the vote, this Conciliation Bill only proposed votes for the richest and most well-educated women. MPs who supported women's suffrage thought this might be the best offer they could get and so would vote in favour.

Others, though, felt their consciences would not allow them to vote for a law that wouldn't include votes for all women, particularly the women of the working class, and so they voted against it. Some political parties worried that these one million women who would be given a vote would all vote for the Conservatives and that their own political party would lose power as a result, so they voted against it, too. And many Irish MPs voted against it because they were having their own problems in Ireland and they wanted the government to focus on that.

But the biggest block to these bills being passed was, once again, the Prime Minister, Mr Asquith. In all, three separate Conciliation Bills were written, in 1910, 1911 and 1912, but none resulted in a law giving women the vote. The failure of the first bill in 1910 in particular was to have devastating consequences.

1910: Black Friday

HOPES WERE HIGH IN EARLY 1910. IT LOOKED AS IF THE GOVERNMENT WAS LISTENING, AND MIGHT FINALLY AGREE TO GIVE AT LEAST SOME WOMEN THE VOTE.

A Conciliation Bill was written. If a majority of MPs approved this bill in Parliament, it would change the law to allow just over one million wealthy, property-owning women the vote. This wasn't ideal, as it completely ignored all working-class women and many middle-class women, too, but both Millicent Fawcett and Emmeline Pankhurst agreed it was better than nothing, and a step in the right direction to one day achieving full suffrage for all women.

A truce was called between the WSPU and the government, and all militant action was stopped. The long, hard battle to win women the vote could soon be over: no more protests; no more prison; no more hunger strikes or force-feeding. Promises had been made, and victory was within reach. Then, right at the last moment, the Prime Minister, Mr Asquith, decided that the Conciliation Bill should be abandoned. The suffragists were right back where they started – with nothing.

All supporters of women's suffrage were extremely upset, but the suffragettes were furious. They felt betrayed by the Prime Minister and decided that on Friday, 18 November 1910, they would march on Parliament in protest and demand to speak with him.

They knew that if they all marched together, they would be arrested immediately, so they agreed to travel in small groups in order to evade the authorities. Everyone knew that the protest was planned, but there was nothing to be done about just a few women walking through the streets together.

Having gathered in Caxton Hall, 300 suffragettes set off in groups of twelve at five-minute intervals on the short march to Parliament. Emmeline Pankhurst led the first group, alongside Princess Sophia Duleep Singh, Elizabeth Garrett Anderson (the UK's first female doctor, who was by then seventy-four years old), her daughter, Louise Garrett Anderson (also a doctor), Hertha Ayrton (an engineer, mathematician and physicist), Dorinda Neligan (a headmistress) and Georgina Solomon (a campaigner for racial and religious equality). Following behind them on horseback was Evelina Haverfield, as some kind of protection for the women on the ground.

Winston Churchill was then Home Secretary, which made him responsible for keeping law and order. The last thing he wanted was a crowd of suffragettes ending up in prison and going on hunger strike, with all the bad publicity that would ensue. So (although he later denied it) in anticipation of the protest, Churchill gave instructions to the police to keep the women away from Parliament and the Prime Minister – but not to make any arrests.

This was a recipe for disaster. Crowds had gathered in Westminster on that Friday, curious to see what might happen. As they approached Parliament Square, Mrs Pankhurst and her leading group were jostled and bumped, but managed to push their way through the crowds to the St Stephen's entrance of the House of Commons. But as they demanded to speak with Mr Asquith, the scene behind them turned nasty.

The following groups of suffragettes, blocked by an army of police (some say as many as 5,000), pushed forward again and again, but could not break through to join Mrs Pankhurst and the leading group.

Behind them the crowd jeered at the women, calling out insults. Some grabbed and snatched their banners, which read 'The Bill, the Whole Bill and Nothing but the Bill', and tore them up, laughing and joking with each other.

Determined that the rest of the suffragettes should not be allowed to join Mrs Pankhurst, the police began breaking up the ever-increasing number arriving in Parliament Square, as if they were breaking up a drunken brawl.

The women found themselves being tossed about like rag dolls, pushed violently and repeatedly back and forth from one policeman to another. Punched, battered, kicked and beaten, some were picked up and flung into the crowds of surrounding men, while others were flung to the ground, dragged down alleys and roughed up.

Helpless, Mrs Pankhurst and her group of (mostly elderly) ladies watched in horror, screaming for the violence to stop, but the fight raged on for six long hours.

Some police had their helmets knocked off in the frenzy, as women were trampled by horses, and in one case pushed in front of a moving car. Evelina Haverfield charged full speed into the battle, striking policemen's faces with her whip, before she was dragged from her horse.

Princess Sophia watched in disbelief as a policeman grabbed a suffragette around her waist and flung her to the ground over and over until she was too weak and dazed to fight back. Sophia ran to the woman's defence, demanding to know the officer's number so she could report him, which she did. But no charges were ever brought against him, or against any of the other policemen who acted with such brutality that day. Eventually the police began arresting people, and over a hundred women and four men were taken to Bow Street police station. All were released without charge the very next day.

The events of 18 November 1910 proved to be a disaster for the government. Many people blamed Winston Churchill, and in the days that followed over a hundred women made official complaints. They described horrible injuries, telling of arms being twisted and thumbs bent back, of punches to the neck and face, and even of having their skirts lifted up above their heads, which would have been particularly humiliating and shocking for them.

Later, the violence the suffragettes experienced that day was often cited as justification for the more extreme forms of protest adopted from 1912. What was the point of women being hurt, when damage to property drew just as much attention to their cause.

The press sided with the suffragettes, and the *Daily Mirror* printed a photograph on its front page of Ada Wright, a suffragette, lying collapsed on the ground. Highly embarrassed, the government tried to stop the paper printing the picture, but it was too late. The story of 'Black Friday', as it became known, was there for the world to see. If the government had hoped to suppress the suffragettes' protest, the very opposite had been achieved.

1910: Suffrajitsu

Fig. 1   Fig. 2   Fig. 3

SHE WAS ONLY FOUR FEET ELEVEN INCHES TALL, BUT EDITH GARRUD COULD THROW A POLICEMAN OVER HER SHOULDER, NO PROBLEM AT ALL. FOR EDITH HAD LEARNED THE ANCIENT MARTIAL ART OF JU-JITSU.

Of course, the suffragettes didn't go around throwing policemen over their shoulders willy-nilly. But after being pushed around so violently and even beaten up by policemen on Black Friday, many suffragettes decided they ought to learn how to defend themselves.

Ju-jitsu (which translated from Japanese means 'soft art') was perfect, being all about defence, not attack. The idea is to knock your attacker off balance, and then use

their body weight to push or fling them to the ground. It is as much a science as a sport. By learning ju-jitsu, a woman, regardless of her size, could easily deflect an attack from a bigger, stronger man.

At the time, there was a craze for all things Japanese. Edith Garrud, along with her husband William, had learned the skill of ju-jitsu from Mr Barton Wright, who had brought two Japanese ju-jitsu masters to Britain. Edith and William ran a martial arts school in London, where Edith would give lessons in self-defence to women and children.

Soon suffragettes started attending, at first to learn how to fend off angry stage invaders and troublemakers at

Fig. 4   Fig. 5   Fig. 6

their speeches and rallies. But after the brutality of Black Friday, Edith began giving special classes exclusively to suffragettes.

Regularly writing for the *Suffragette* newspaper on the subject, with photographs and diagrams illustrating how to do the moves, Edith would describe the art of 'twisting wrists, elbows or knee joints the way they are not meant to go'. Ouch!

A woman doing any sort of physical activity would have been a curiosity to many at this time, so a tiny policeman-throwing lady in huge hat and long skirt caused a bit of a stir. Edith became quite famous, and cartoons were drawn of her fending off big burly brutes or hurling policemen over railings, while others stood quivering nearby. Poems were written about her:

> For women are learning ju-jitsu,
> And throwing policemen about;
> And when a man meets
> With the women athletes
> He'll have to be good – or get out.

Before long, journalists had coined the phrases 'Ju-jit-suffragettes' and 'Suffrajitsu'.

It sounds comical, but shows the determination and preparedness of the suffragettes.

1911: The Suffragette in the Broom Cupboard

EMILY WILDING DAVISON WAS CLEVER. SHE WAS DETERMINED TO BREAK THE RULES MADE BY THE GOVERNMENT UNTIL THEY GAVE WOMEN THE VOTE. AND SHE WAS VERY GOOD AT BREAKING RULES.

The year 1911 was a 'census' year. A census is a way for the government to count how many people there are in the country and where they live. Absolutely everyone must be included, so every ten years since 1841 the head of every household has had to fill out a form and write the names of all the people who are living there or visiting on that particular census night.

This way the government gets a good picture of the whole population and can make decisions on things like healthcare and education. It is against the law to refuse to fill out a census form or to mess it up by writing 'VOTES FOR WOMEN' across it or 'IF WOMEN DON'T COUNT, NEITHER SHALL THEY BE COUNTED'. But that is exactly what some suffragettes did in 1911. This was very brave, as they faced a fine or even prison by doing it.

Some suffragettes found other ways to commit acts of civil disobedience. Up and down the whole country, many decided to avoid being at home for the census, and spent the night walking the streets. Some camped out on Wimbledon Common, others went to all-night concerts that were being specially held to encourage women to avoid the census. Many walked round and round Trafalgar Square, and some restaurants stayed open all night so the women could stop for a cup of tea to keep up their energy.

Some suffragettes declared their homes to be a 'census-avoiding property' where no forms would be filled in. They invited women to stay the night, and some had twenty-five or more sleeping in their house. One resilient suffragette put on her winter coat and sat all night in her garden shed.

All this was to purposely mess up the government's system of getting information on the population.

Emily Wilding Davison had an even more brilliant idea: to hide in a broom cupboard in the Chapel of the Palace of Westminster (the building that houses Parliament).

And she did just that. Emily hid there until morning, with only some meat lozenges to snack on and lime juice to drink.

It sounds horrible, but by spending the night of 2 April 1911 in that cupboard, she could officially write on her census form that her place of residence was the Houses of Parliament. The 1911 census actually lists Emily Wilding Davidson (they spelled her name wrong) as 'found hiding in crypt of Westminster Hall'.

What a clever idea. Although women were not allowed to vote or to become MPs, through her actions, she knew her name would forever be linked to the Houses of Parliament.

Sadly, however, the name Emily Wilding Davison would be best remembered for a tragic event that took place two years later, as the suffragettes continued to find new ways to protest.

1911: Acid, Ink and Fire Bombs

BY 1911 THE SUPPORTERS OF WOMEN'S SUFFRAGE WERE THOROUGHLY FED UP. THEY FELT IGNORED BY THE GOVERNMENT – AND BY EVERYONE ELSE, FOR THAT MATTER. THEY NEEDED TO DO SOMETHING EXTREME.

Some members of the WSPU decided to take matters into their own hands, and across the country attacks started to take place on, of all things, postboxes.

Postboxes made eye-catching targets. In the early 1900s, there were no computers, no Internet, and very few people owned a telephone; there was certainly no such thing as a mobile phone. Writing letters was the only way to communicate, which made the Royal Mail a precious and vital part of everyday life; people depended on it. It is said that in those days you could receive a letter, write and post your response, and even receive a reply, all on the same day. The suffragettes knew exactly what they were doing by destroying the mail. These post-box attacks were designed to wake up the public and the government, and force them to take seriously the question of women's suffrage.

Some postboxes were set on fire, and many more had ink or acid poured into them to destroy the letters inside. The very first time a postbox was set ablaze was in December 1911, when Emily Wilding Davison set not one, but three postboxes on fire. Other suffragettes followed her example. Margaret Haig Thomas (the 2nd Viscountess Rhondda), known as 'The Welsh Boadicea', from the Newport branch of the WSPU in Wales, tried to blow up a postbox with a home-made bomb. She was arrested, as was Rosa May Billinghurst for the same offence. Rosa never let her wheelchair get in the way of being an active militant suffragette, and decorated her chair in the colours of the WSPU, with banners and ribbons proclaiming 'VOTES FOR WOMEN'. She was arrested several times.

Emily, Margaret and Rosa were all sent to prison, and they all went on hunger strike. Many people were enraged by these acts, which they saw as a blatant disregard for their important post. They thought the militant suffragettes were a menace, favouring the 'Lock 'em up and throw away the key' approach.

At first, the leaders of the WSPU did not want to be seen to support such destruction by individual members of their organization, but it wasn't long before they were given the seal of approval by Emmeline Pankhurst herself. In 1912 she gave a big speech at the Royal Albert Hall in London in which she encouraged her supporters to 'be militant in [their] own way' and to do whatever they could to force the government to give votes to women. This was just the start of the assault against property.

1912: A Bigger Smash

IN 1912, WINDOW SMASHING BECAME OFFICIALLY APPROVED BY THE LEADERS OF THE WSPU.

Back in 1908, when Mary Leigh and Edith New had smashed the windows of Number 10 Downing Street, it had been very much an individual action. But by 1912, the breaking of windows had become organized, with coordinated attacks designed to cause as much damage and disruption as possible.

In 1911, MPs voted in favour of the Second Conciliation Bill, which would give over one million women the vote. But before it could be made law, Prime Minister Asquith again interfered, and changed it into a 'Manhood Suffrage' bill, which instead focused on giving the vote to the millions of working-class men who still had no right to one. The women were angry to have been written out of the bill, and on 21 November they organized a massive window-breaking attack.

The sound of breaking glass could be heard coming from government buildings all over London, but this time some shops, hotels, newspaper offices and gentlemen's clubs were attacked too. Over two hundred women and three men were arrested and sent to prison, and hundreds of pounds' worth of damage was reported.

Many suffragettes did not agree with window breaking, believing it was losing them support from the public,

and left the WSPU to join other, non-militant suffrage groups. But Emmeline Pankhurst wasn't bothered in the slightest, declaring, 'The smashing of windows is a time-honoured method of showing displeasure in a political situation.'

On 1 March 1912 at precisely 5.30 in the afternoon, elegantly dressed ladies whipped out miniature toffee hammers from their muffs and handbags and proceeded to calmly smash shop windows in London. Up and down Oxford Street, Regent Street and the Strand came the piercing sound of metal hitting glass, followed by the angry shouts of shoppers and shopkeepers.

The WSPU were insistent that no one should get injured in the attack, so the women were instructed how to break the glass so that it wouldn't rain splinters and shards down on themselves or on passers-by.

Emmeline Pankhurst and her friend Ethel Smyth both took part, and were among the 126 women arrested. The cost of all that broken glass came to over £5,000 (worth about £400,000 today), and for days afterwards some of the fanciest shops in London had boarded-up windows. Some smaller shops even put up signs in their windows, begging the suffragettes not to smash them. Once again, the public were getting fed up. But women like Emmeline and Ethel were not about to give up the fight.

1912: 'Shout, Shout, Up With Your Song!'

ETHEL SMYTH LOVED GOLF AND COULD OFTEN BE SEEN ON THE GOLF COURSE DRESSED HEAD TO TOE IN TWEED, WITH HER HAT ON WONKY. IT WAS MUSIC, HOWEVER, THAT WAS HER LIFE.

Ethel lived for music: the rhythm of it, the power of it, the conversations between notes. Her father had been dead set against her becoming a composer, but that didn't stop his daughter. It just made her more determined. She studied hard and wrote all sorts of music, including many operas, and became famous around the world.

Then in 1910, she met Emmeline Pankhurst and fell head over heels in love with her. She was so captivated by Emmeline's zeal for victory in winning the vote for women that Ethel declared she would give up her musical career for two whole years and instead dedicate that time to the WSPU. She joined up immediately and soon put her talents to good use by writing the song that would become the WSPU's anthem; not just a song, but 'a hymn and a call to battle': 'The March of the Women'.

There is something very special about singing in a group. To raise your voice in song creates a magical feeling and a sense of belonging together. I guess this is why people sing at football matches or in church. You don't even need to be a good singer, as you can mingle your voice with the others and still make a joyful noise.

The suffragettes loved to sing together. It made them feel connected in their struggle to win the vote. And there was no better song than 'The March of the Women' to make them feel good about themselves. The lyrics, written by Cicely Hamilton, speak of fearlessness and strength, bravery and glory: inspiring words to keep spirits high.

In 1912, encouraged by Emmeline, Ethel threw a stone through the window of a leading politician opposed to women's suffrage, and was promptly arrested. She was sentenced to two months in Holloway Prison. A visiting friend remembered watching the other suffragette prisoners parading around the prison yard singing with gusto their 'war chant', 'The March of the Women', while above them from her cell window Ethel enthusiastically conducted with a toothbrush.

The following year, Ethel started to go deaf, which meant she could no longer compose music. Instead she wrote books, but her contribution to music was remembered when in 1922 she became the first female composer to be made a Dame.

The March of the Women.

Dedicated to the Women's Social and Political Union

PRICE ONE PENNY ETHEL SMYTH. Mus. Doc.

(Band)

1. Shout, shout, up with your song! Cry with the wind, for the dawn is break-ing.

March, march, swing you a–long, Wide blows our ban-ner and hope is wak-ing. Song with its sto-ry, dreams with their glo-ry,

Lo! They call and glad is their word. For-ward!

Hark how it swells, Thun-der of free-dom, the voice of the Lord!

2.

Long, long, we in the past,
Cowered in dread from the light of Heaven.
Strong, strong stand we at last,
Fearless in faith and with sight new given.
Strength with its beauty, life with its duty,
(Hear the voice, oh, hear and obey).
These, these beckon us on,
Open your eyes to the blaze of day!

3.

Comrades, ye who have dared.
First in the battle to strive and sorrow.
Scorned, spurned, naught have ye cared,
Raising your eyes to a wider morrow.
Ways that are weary, days that are dreary,
Toil and pain by faith ye have borne.
Hail, hail, victors ye stand,
Wearing the wreath that the brave have worn!

4.

Life, strife, these two are one!
Naught can ye win but by faith and daring.
On, on, that ye have done,
But for the work of today preparing.
Firm in reliance, laugh a defiance,
(Laugh in hope, for sure is the end).
March, march, many as one,
Shoulder to shoulder and friend to friend!

1913: A Game of Cat and Mouse

ORCIBLE FEEDING WAS NOT ONLY HUGELY UNPOPULAR WITH THE PUBLIC AND POLITICIANS, BUT IT WAS NOT REALLY WORKING.

The suffragette prisoners were ever more determined to stand united in their struggle, and more and more women and men were joining in the hunger strike as soon as they were imprisoned.

Terrified of the backlash from the public should a suffragette die in prison, the government came up with their sneakiest tactic yet. In April 1913, a new law was hurriedly passed. It was called the 'Temporary Discharge for Ill Health Act'.

But here is why it was so sneaky. A prisoner would be allowed to go on hunger strike, refusing food and even water, until they became weak and ill. Then they would be released from jail and allowed to go home or to stay in a safehouse for, say, two weeks or longer.

At home they would begin eating normally once more, and in time regain their health and strength, at which point the prisoner would be expected to return to prison and complete their sentence. Of course, no one ever went back to prison voluntarily. Once out, the

suffragettes did their very best to stay out; some went into hiding, while others even left the country.

The police had to keep watch over released prisoners, spying on their every move, ready to pounce and re-arrest them when their health had improved.

What a dreadfully dreary process. A prison sentence of a couple of months could be stretched out over a year or more, with the prisoner constantly yo-yoing back and forth to jail, threatening their physical and mental well-being.

This law became known as 'The Cat and Mouse Act'. The government was like a cat playing with its prey, a suffragette, or the mouse: trapping it, letting it go, then pouncing on it again and again until the poor mouse was too weak to fight back.

The WSPU released a poster showing an illustration of a mean-looking cat with blood-stained fangs. In its jaws hung the limp, listless body of a suffragette (the mouse), draped in the purple, green and white colours of the Union. It was a very powerful and sinister image.

The first prisoner to be released under the Act was not officially a suffragette, but a man called Hugh Franklin.

Prisoners (Temporary Discharge for Ill-health) Act, 1913

AN ACT

TO

Provide for the Temporary Discharge of Prisoners whose further detention in prison is undesirable on account of the condition of their Health.

25th April 1913

Hugh was from a very rich family. He was at Cambridge University studying engineering, but he gave up his studies after hearing Mrs Pankhurst, Mrs Pethick-Lawrence and Christabel Pankhurst speaking at his college in 1909.

Hugh was already a firm believer in women's equality, but after this encounter with 'the Militants', he decided to dedicate all his time to joining them in acts of civil disobedience.

Being a man, he wasn't allowed to join the WSPU, so he joined the Men's Political Union for Women's Enfranchisement and the Men's League for Women's Suffrage. He also helped form the Jewish League for Women's Suffrage.

He was one of the four men arrested on Black Friday, although on that occasion he wasn't sent to jail. Hugh blamed Winston Churchill for the violence and abuse the suffragettes received that day, and later attacked Churchill with a whip. For that, he did go to prison.

In total, Hugh went to jail three times in support of winning votes for women. The second time was for throwing a stone at Churchill's house, and the third was for setting fire to a railway carriage at Harrow station.

For that, he got nine months in jail and went on hunger strike. Hugh was force-fed over a hundred times before the government released him under the Cat and Mouse Act.

The second person to be released just so happened to be Hugh's girlfriend, Elise Duval. Elise was from a family of keen suffragists and had been in jail for loitering. On hunger strike, she was force-fed nine times before being released in very poor health. Elise and Hugh ran off to Belgium to avoid being re-arrested, and didn't return to Britain for over a year.

Cruel as it was, however, even the Cat and Mouse Act did nothing to pause the fight for votes for women.

1913: Capturing the Monument

UNDAUNTED BY THE GOVERNMENT'S CRUEL TACTICS, THE SUFFRAGETTES FOUND INCREASINGLY INVENTIVE WAYS OF BRINGING ATTENTION TO THEIR FIGHT.

By acting in secret, they continued to outwit the police who were constantly taken by surprise, even when major events or landmarks were targeted.

On the morning of Friday, 18 April 1913, Ethel Spark and Gertrude Shaw each bought themselves a ticket to go up the Monument in London, the tower built to commemorate the Great Fire of London in 1666.

Together they climbed the 311 steps to the top, where they politely chatted with the two attendants on duty that day.

While the men were distracted, the women managed to trap them in their office and slammed shut the door to the viewing platform, locking it tight with two iron poles that they had smuggled in under their clothes.

Then, quick as a flash, they hauled down the City of London flag that was flying high on the flagpole, and replaced it with the purple, green and white flag of the WSPU.

Next, a large banner that read 'Death or Victory' in huge letters was unfurled over the railings, along with streamers of purple, green and white that billowed in the breeze.

When a large enough crowd had gathered to see what all the fuss was about, Ethel and Gertrude let loose hundreds of 'Votes for Women' leaflets that fluttered down to the streets below.

Eventually, the police arrived, but they needed an enormous sledgehammer to break down the door. It took some time, but eventually they reached the women and arrested them.

Ethel and Gertrude were taken to Bow Street Magistrates' Court, but were released without charge. Perhaps the magistrate felt it was not worth the trouble of putting these two annoying women in prison, especially if they were then to go on hunger strike.

It was another successful publicity stunt by the WSPU, who were delighted with themselves for causing such disruption. The Votes for Women newspaper reported the incident with glee as another success 'to add to the list of triumphs of female ingenuity'.

But the members of the NUWSS were impatient with the WSPU. All the violence and destruction caused by a few militant suffragettes was making the public and the government angry and was not, they felt, helping the cause.

Most of the women and men trying to win the vote were law-abiding suffragists, not law-breaking suffragettes, but the law-breakers were getting all the attention.

Something big needed to be done to show the country that not everyone was smashing windows, blowing up postboxes, or locking up attendants in the name of women's suffrage.

In fact some suffragists believed that 'words' would in the end prove more effective than 'deeds' when it came to winning the vote.

1913: The Pilgrims Make Progress

QUITE BY COINCIDENCE, ON THE VERY SAME DAY AS THE WSPU WERE STORMING THE MONUMENT, THE NUWSS WERE PLANNING THEIR OWN, PEACEFUL, PUBLICITY CAMPAIGN.

The Scottish suffragists had had their own march from Edinburgh to London in 1912, and in the summer of 1913 it was decided that an even bigger pilgrimage of women would march from all corners of England and Wales, from Land's End to Newcastle, to meet at Hyde Park in London.

Starting from the furthermost districts on 18 and 19 June, groups of women and a small number of men set off from seventeen towns and cities.

It would take weeks to walk that far, and the NUWSS encouraged as many of its 100,000 members as possible to take part, but they were not expected to walk the whole route, just to join in for chunks of it, to show a steady, strong troop. Some rode bicycles, others rode horses, but the pilgrimage was not supposed to be a big, showy carnival parade. Quite the opposite: this was about talking to people along the way.

Even so, they wanted to be recognized by the public, so they wore a sort of uniform: white, grey, black or navy skirts, with matching blouses, and hats decorated in the red, green and white of the NUWSS. It was a simple uniform, so that any member of the Union could join in without having to buy a new outfit.

The pilgrimage was a brilliant idea. The suffragists were able to chat with people face to face, discussing their thoughts and ideas about women's suffrage as they passed through the towns and villages on their journey.

It was mostly friendly; sometimes the whole town would turn out to see the suffragists and cheer them on. Little children would present them with posies of flowers, and the atmosphere was inquisitive and jolly.

Not everyone was so welcoming, though. As they passed through some towns, the women were pelted with stones, eggs, mud, and even great big cabbages. They had their hats ripped off, were pushed off their bikes, and had their luggage thrown in rivers. In some towns, groups of working-class men protected the women from being mobbed by hooligans, including university students who considered these women a joke. Not having the vote themselves yet, these working men were more sympathetic to the cause.

When they reached Hyde Park on 26 July, they were dusty, sunburned and tired, but in a triumphant mood. The pilgrimage had been a huge success. They had collected over £8,000 (worth about £650,000 today) for the Union, given out half a million leaflets, and enrolled thousands of new members.

The NUWSS seemed to be back on track for victory. And without recourse to the violence or law-breaking of the WSPU, which still continued.

1913: Burning Down the House

ON 3 MARCH 1912, A MIDWIFE CALLED ELLEN PITFIELD SET FIRE TO A BASKET OF WOOD IN A POST OFFICE.

She then threw a brick through its window – and so began the next and most devastatingly destructive phase of the WSPU's campaign of protest against the government's unwillingness to bring about political change.

Emmeline Pankhurst had called upon the suffragettes to destroy the one thing that in her opinion men valued the most: property. She also made very clear that no human life should be harmed in such attacks, writing, 'I have never advised the destruction of life, but of property, YES!'

At first the homes of leading anti-suffragists were targeted, but before long all sorts of public and private property went up in flames at the strike of a match lit by a suffragette. Often while investigating the smouldering ruins, police would find little notes reading 'votes for women' or 'stop torturing our comrades in prison', which left little doubt as to who the attackers had been.

A theatre in Dublin where the Prime Minister Henry Herbert Asquith was due to give a speech was attacked by Mary Leigh and Gladys Evans, and although only the curtain went up in smoke, they each received a prison sentence of five years.

By 1913, rail carriages had been set ablaze, the orchid house at Kew Gardens burned to the ground, an Oxford boathouse, a cricket pavilion, and a racecourse grandstand all destroyed or damaged by fire. On 26 December 1913, *The Suffragette* listed over one hundred of the more serious attacks on property that had taken place that year and had been attributed to the suffragettes.

Suffragettes had even attempted to blow up a country house that was being built for David Lloyd George, who as Chancellor of the Exchequer was an important member of the government.

Emmeline Pankhurst claimed full responsibility for inciting the bombers. This time she was sentenced to three years in jail.

The suffragettes were attracting more and more attention, including from the authorities. The headquarters of the WSPU was raided by police, and 'troublemaker' suffragettes were put under surveillance.

Some suffragettes, including Christabel Pankhurst, had escaped to Paris when they were released from jail under the Cat and Mouse Act. They could not be allowed to beat the system in this way, so by the end of the year, force-feeding was reintroduced for hunger-striking prisoners. Meanwhile, any sympathy the public had for the suffragettes was fast running out.

1913: A Death at the Races

EMILY WILDING DAVISON WAS FIERCE AND FEARLESS. AS A MEMBER OF THE WSPU, SHE DEDICATED YEARS OF HER LIFE TO THE CAMPAIGN TO WIN VOTES FOR WOMEN.

She was a bit of a loose cannon. A dedicated risk-taker, Emily would, it seemed, do anything in the fight for women's suffrage. This irked the leaders of the WSPU, who had on occasions tried to distance themselves from her more extreme actions.

In 1909 she quit her job as a teacher to become a full-time warrior suffragette. She threw stones, smashed windows, set fire to things. She once attacked a church minister, mistaking him for David Lloyd George, then Chancellor of the Exchequer and a senior member of the government. Some people think she even planted a bomb in his 'empty' house.

Emily Davison went to prison nine times, where she joined the hunger strike, and was brutally force-fed. On one occasion, she barricaded herself into her cell to avoid force-feeding, and was hosed down with freezing cold water until she felt like she was drowning. Once she threw herself down the iron stairs in the prison to deliberately hurt herself and bring attention to the plight of her fellow hunger strikers. But no one, not even her closest friends, could imagine what she would do next.

The Epsom Derby: one of the most splendid and important races of the year for any horse-racing fan. On 4 June 1913, thousands of spectators were gathered to watch, among them Emily Wilding Davison.

Just before the race began, Emily found herself a spot with a great view right at the front of the crowd on the bend known as Tattenham Corner. She had two suffragette flags hidden in her clothing and, folded neatly in her left hand, a silk scarf in the purple, green and white colours of the WSPU, imprinted with the motto 'Votes for Women'.

As the horses thundered towards her, she calmly ducked under the barrier and quite deliberately walked right out on to the racetrack. Emily stood facing the horses as they sped past, her eyes fixed on one horse in particular: Amner, the King's horse.

She raised her arms as Amner hurtled towards her. King George V, Queen Mary and hundreds of spectators watched in horror as the horse suddenly collided with Emily, who was tossed head over heels, tumbling through the air. Such was the force of the impact that Amner also somersaulted, catapulting his jockey, Herbert Jones, from his back. The horse crashed to the ground, then stumbled back to his feet unharmed.

Emily and Herbert lay motionless on the track as the race continued. People rushed forward to help, and the two were taken to hospital.

Herbert, who wasn't very badly injured, made a full recovery, but Emily never regained consciousness: her skull had been fractured, and she died of her injuries four days later.

At the time, most people thought Emily had purposely tried to kill herself by trying to grab hold of the King's horse in a crazy publicity stunt. But many historians think differently now, and don't believe she had intended to die. Of course we will never know for sure, but the folded silk scarf in her hand could be a clue to her real intentions. One thought is that she was attempting to throw the scarf over the neck of the horse as it charged past her: the sight of the King's horse crossing the finishing line draped in a suffragette scarf emblazoned with the words 'Votes for Women' would have been the greatest publicity stunt the suffragettes had ever achieved. Perhaps Emily simply misjudged the speed of the galloping horse, or her own position on the track.

Whatever the truth, there is no doubt Emily wanted to draw maximum attention to the campaign for women's votes. The race was being filmed, and she managed to place herself in the perfect spot to be captured on camera. By the end of the day, blurry black-and-white images of her actions were flickering across cinema screens all over the country.

Her funeral procession through the streets of London was a tremendous spectacle watched by thousands, both those crowding the streets as it passed, and those in cinemas watching the newsreel footage.

Emily Wilding Davison had become the most famous suffragette in the world.

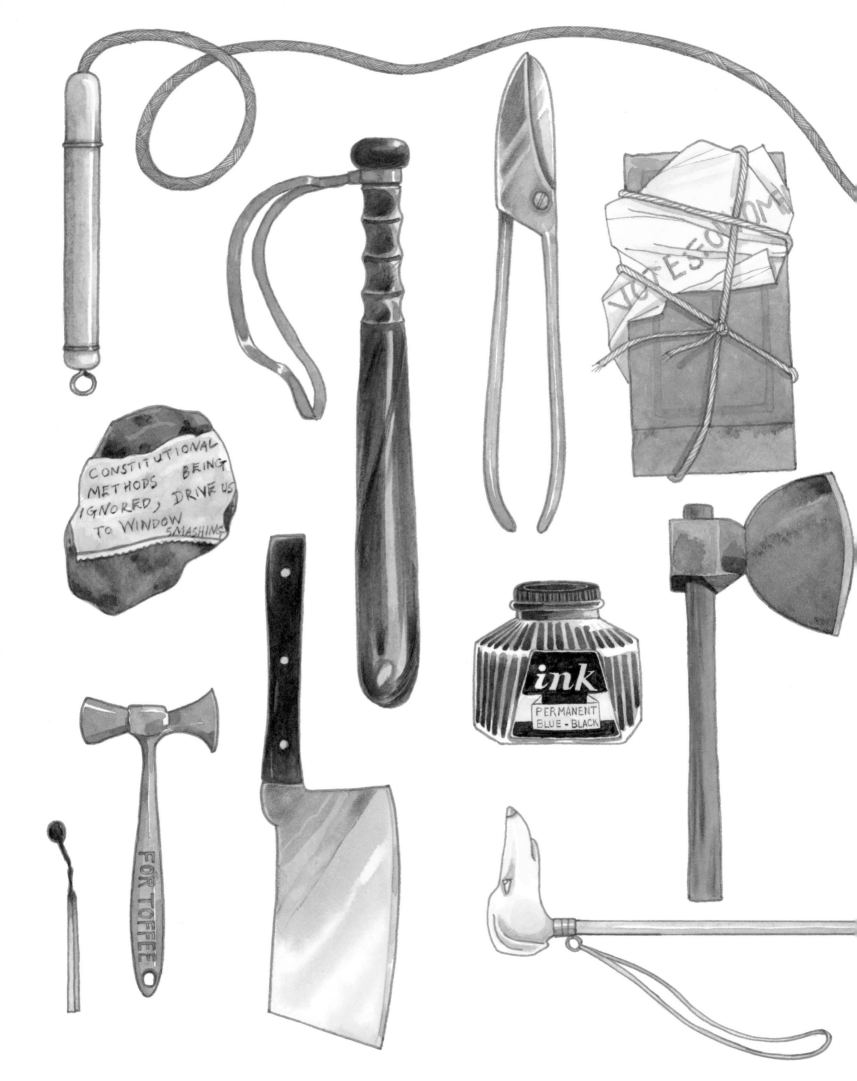

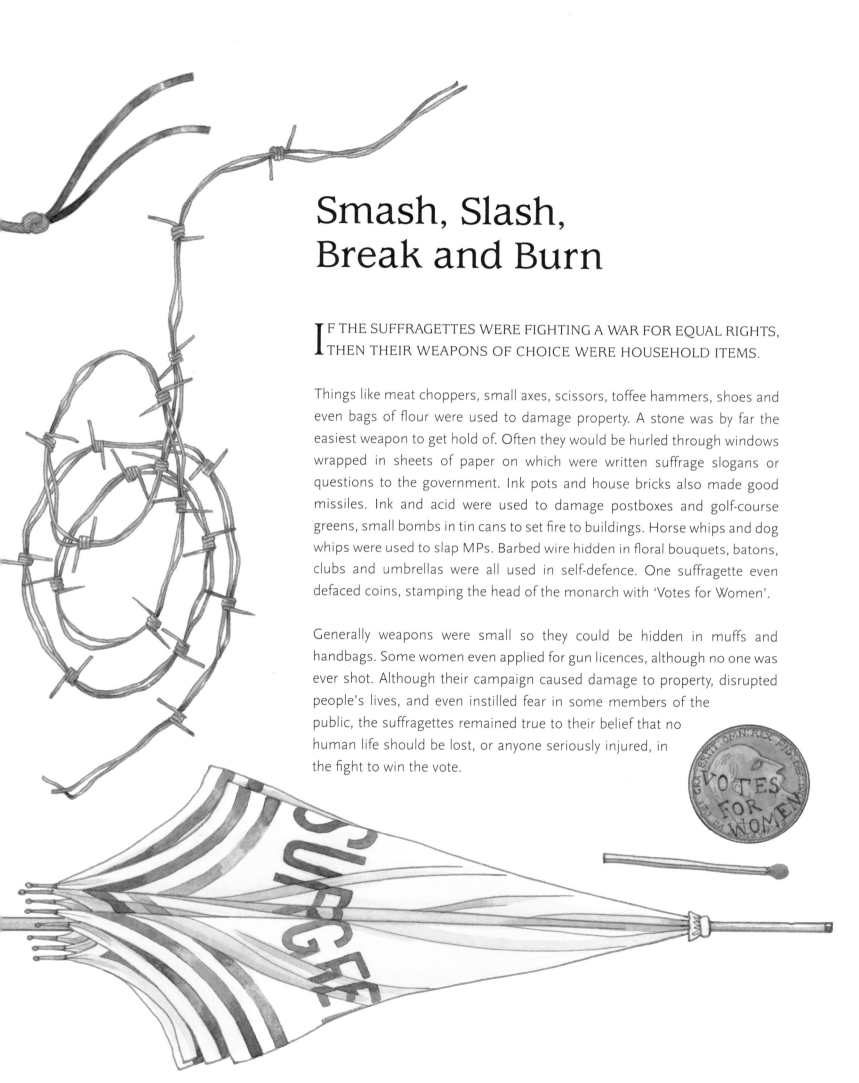

Smash, Slash, Break and Burn

I F THE SUFFRAGETTES WERE FIGHTING A WAR FOR EQUAL RIGHTS, THEN THEIR WEAPONS OF CHOICE WERE HOUSEHOLD ITEMS.

Things like meat choppers, small axes, scissors, toffee hammers, shoes and even bags of flour were used to damage property. A stone was by far the easiest weapon to get hold of. Often they would be hurled through windows wrapped in sheets of paper on which were written suffrage slogans or questions to the government. Ink pots and house bricks also made good missiles. Ink and acid were used to damage postboxes and golf-course greens, small bombs in tin cans to set fire to buildings. Horse whips and dog whips were used to slap MPs. Barbed wire hidden in floral bouquets, batons, clubs and umbrellas were all used in self-defence. One suffragette even defaced coins, stamping the head of the monarch with 'Votes for Women'.

Generally weapons were small so they could be hidden in muffs and handbags. Some women even applied for gun licences, although no one was ever shot. Although their campaign caused damage to property, disrupted people's lives, and even instilled fear in some members of the public, the suffragettes remained true to their belief that no human life should be lost, or anyone seriously injured, in the fight to win the vote.

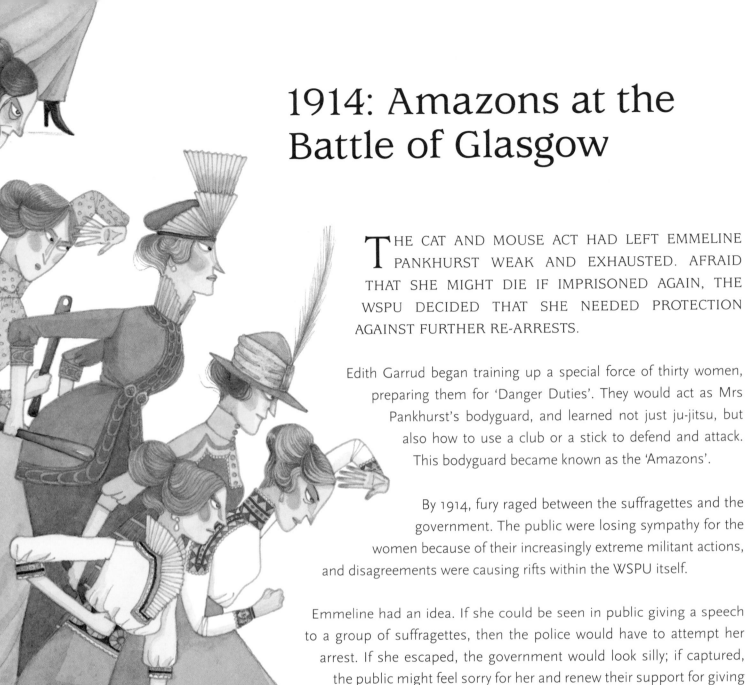

1914: Amazons at the Battle of Glasgow

THE CAT AND MOUSE ACT HAD LEFT EMMELINE PANKHURST WEAK AND EXHAUSTED. AFRAID THAT SHE MIGHT DIE IF IMPRISONED AGAIN, THE WSPU DECIDED THAT SHE NEEDED PROTECTION AGAINST FURTHER RE-ARRESTS.

Edith Garrud began training up a special force of thirty women, preparing them for 'Danger Duties'. They would act as Mrs Pankhurst's bodyguard, and learned not just ju-jitsu, but also how to use a club or a stick to defend and attack. This bodyguard became known as the 'Amazons'.

By 1914, fury raged between the suffragettes and the government. The public were losing sympathy for the women because of their increasingly extreme militant actions, and disagreements were causing rifts within the WSPU itself.

Emmeline had an idea. If she could be seen in public giving a speech to a group of suffragettes, then the police would have to attempt her arrest. If she escaped, the government would look silly; if captured, the public might feel sorry for her and renew their support for giving women the vote.

A suffragette meeting was to be held in March 1914 at St Andrew's Hall in Glasgow. Rumours abounded that Emmeline, who was in hiding after her most recent release from prison under the Cat and Mouse Act, would be there to make a speech.

The venue was jam-packed. The police were taking no chances of letting Mrs Pankhurst slip through their fingers and had surrounded the building. Fifty more police were hiding in the basement below. It seemed impossible that Emmeline could slink past them unnoticed.

But just when all hope of hearing Mrs Pankhurst speak that day was fading, Emmeline miraculously appeared on stage. It was not a miracle, or even a clever magic trick; she had simply worn a disguise, bought a ticket like everyone else, and swished into the Hall right under the noses of the waiting police. To the delight of the audience, she began her speech:

'Equal justice for men and women, equal political justice, equal legal justice, equal industrial justice and equal social justice! . . .'

But her speech was cut short by the ominous sound of the police rushing up from the basement. One of the Amazons whipped out a pistol and shots rang out. Fortunately, they were blanks. Startled but uninjured, the police stumbled their way to the stage. Twenty-five Amazons formed a circle around Mrs Pankhurst, armed with the sticks and clubs they had hidden in their dresses.

The first policeman to clamber on to the platform was ensnared and tangled in the barbed wire hidden by the suffragettes among the pretty floral garlands decorating the stage. Several plain-clothes policemen were hiding in the audience and they now made a move to grab Mrs Pankhurst, but were beaten back by ladies with umbrellas. The crowd booed and jeered as the police walloped the Amazons with their truncheons. Chairs and tables were flung about as the battle raged on.

They put up a brave fight, but the Amazons were soon overpowered by the police, and Emmeline was captured and dragged from the Hall, tattered and bruised from the struggle. The government was victorious; Mrs Pankhurst was back in prison.

But the public were appalled. Emmeline had been right. After what became known as the Battle of Glasgow, people once again renewed their sympathy and support for the fight to win women the vote.

1914: Don't Forget the Workers

POSH LADIES THROWING STONES IS THE POPULAR IMAGE OF WHO THE SUFFRAGETTES WERE, BUT THAT IS JUST ONE SIDE OF THE WHOLE SUFFRAGE CAMPAIGN.

Thousands of suffragettes and suffragists were working-class people, some from extremely poor backgrounds. These women didn't have much money or free time, but they gave a great deal of support to the fight for their rights for a better life.

Some of the suffrage organizations were concerned only with winning the right for women to vote on equal terms with men. Not all men had the vote, however, so in 1914 that meant only upper- and middle-class women who were well educated or who owned their own home would be given the right to vote.

Working-class women were rightly disgruntled. They wanted votes for *all* women and men, regardless of class, education or wealth. They risked a great deal by being involved with the suffragists, and particularly with the suffragettes.

Many of the poorest working women would only get one day off work a week, but they would give up that day to join in with protest marches and processions. A working-class woman involved in a skirmish with the police could lose her job and face destitution as a result. Poor women who were arrested would never be able to afford to pay a fine, so would inevitably end up being sent to prison. Sometimes these women might be the only person in their household bringing home a wage, and so prison could mean their children went without proper food and care for months, not to mention the shame and rejection they faced from their communities or families, many of whom disapproved of their actions.

But many working-class women knew that the change that was needed to help them take control of their own lives would only come about when women played a part in politics and had an equal voice in governing the country. At the beginning of the 1900s, nearly 30,000 working women from the North-West textile factories and mills had signed a petition demanding better pay and working conditions. This is what had prompted Emmeline Pankhurst to create the WSPU in the first place.

But by 1914, the increasingly violent and extreme militant actions of certain members of the WSPU were causing squabbles and disapproval between the different suffrage organizations. The WSPU, which had started as a union to support working women's rights, had broadened to attract women of all social classes, rich and poor, since all women were excluded from the exercise of the parliamentary vote. Emmeline and Christabel also insisted that the WSPU should be independent and not allied to any of the men's political parties of the day, including the Labour Party, even though they were more sympathetic to the cause of votes for women.

Sylvia Pankhurst – Emmeline's younger daughter – did not agree with this approach, instead wanting to ally the WSPU more closely to the socialist movement. She formed her own group, the East London Federation of the Suffragettes (ELFS). The ELFS, contrary to WSPU policy, included both women and men members and supported Labour Party candidates who stood for election to parliament.

In January 1914, Sylvia was expelled from the WSPU because she had dared to disagree with her mother Emmeline and sister Christabel. Along with Minnie Lansbury, Melvina Walker and Julia Scurr, Sylvia refocused on the social issues affecting poor women.

VOTES FOR WORKERS

1914: 'Slasher' Mary and the Art Attacks

MARY RICHARDSON LOVED ART, WHICH AT FIRST GLANCE MAKES WHAT SHE DID SEEM VERY STRANGE INDEED.

On 10 March 1914, Mary went to the National Gallery in London. There was one particular painting she wanted to see: *Venus at her Mirror* by Diego Velázquez, painted in 1647. The gallery had only just bought it, for the then enormous sum of £45,000.

One year earlier, two suffragettes had attacked fourteen paintings at Manchester Art Gallery, smashing their glass and frames.

The National Gallery was taking no chances with its new purchase: two security guards were positioned next to the painting, which was put behind a thick panel of glass for extra protection.

Mary stood in front of the painting, pretending to draw it in a sketchbook. Hidden up her sleeve she had a meat chopper. But the two guards were not budging, and she began to think she would have no chance of getting close enough to attack the picture.

Then, to her surprise, suddenly one of the guards got up and wandered off for his lunch. At the same time, the other guard got out a newspaper and began to read it. With his face hidden by the paper, he didn't notice as Mary stepped forward and took a violent swing at the *Venus*. The meat chopper shattered the protecting glass.

Mary thought she would instantly be grabbed by the newspaper-reading guard, but instead he walked off, looking up at the skylight above, wrongly thinking the window had been smashed.

Mary seized her chance and got in 'five lovely shots' with the chopper, slashing the canvas across the back and shoulders of Venus's body.

Another guard now realized what was happening and ran to stop her, but he slipped on the polished floor and fell flat on his face. Mary couldn't believe her luck. She got in a few more slashes before she was eventually grabbed and arrested. But the painting had been severely damaged.

People were utterly disgusted and appalled, horrified that someone would want to destroy art.

Mary was indignant, and responded, 'I have tried to destroy the picture of the most beautiful woman in mythological history as a protest against the government for destroying Mrs Pankhurst, who is the most beautiful character in modern history . . . You can get another picture, but you cannot get another life . . . They are killing Mrs Pankhurst.'

Later that year, things reached boiling point. Just being seen in the purple, green and white could get a suffragette attacked by a raging member of the public. And if you were a man who supported votes for women, you could find yourself being ducked in a pond or lake, which is exactly what happened to the Reverend C. A. Wills after he had heckled Lloyd George.

But by August 1914, an even greater threat was looming.

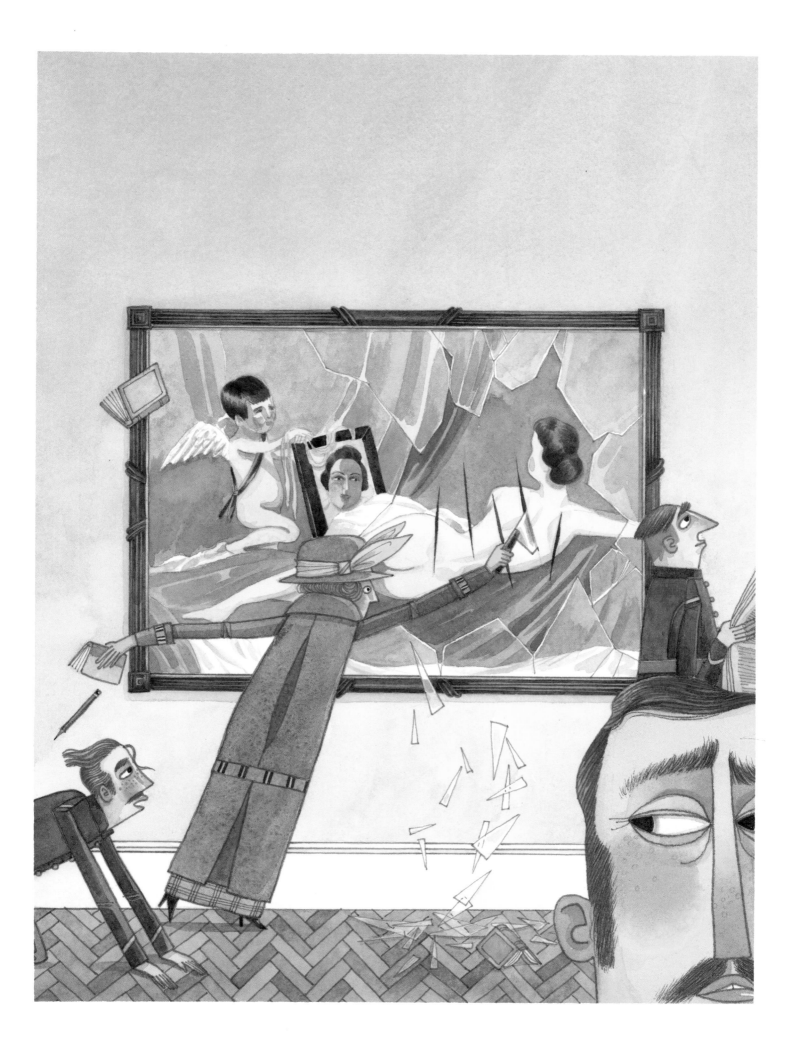

4 AUGUST 1914

The darkness of war descended as Britain began its bloody conflict with Germany.

Almost overnight, the whole campaign for women's suffrage changed, and the violent militant actions of the suffragettes came to an abrupt end.

By 6 August, Millicent Fawcett and the leaders of the NUWSS had pledged their support for the war. Millicent urged its members to 'prove themselves worthy of citizenship, whether our claim (as women) to it be recognized or not'.

By 10 August, the government agreed an amnesty with the WSPU, releasing all suffrage prisoners, in jail or out

(under the Cat and Mouse Act), from their sentences. Suddenly the campaign to win the vote took second place to the more urgent campaign to win the war.

Emmeline Pankhurst wholeheartedly supported the war and urged the members of the WSPU to do the same, declaring: 'What is the use of fighting for a vote if we have not got a country to vote in?'

By the middle of September 1914, over a quarter of a million men had joined up to fight in France and Belgium. The newspaper *Votes for Women* announced: 'Work of all kinds will want doing, and women will have to do it.'

1914: The White Feather Brigade

WINNING THE WAR BECAME THE FOCUS FOR MOST SUFFRAGE GROUPS; WINNING THE VOTE WOULD HAVE TO WAIT.

But not all of the suffrage societies supported the war. The WFL and ELFS both disapproved.

Many of their members were pacifists who believed they should campaign for peace, while continuing to strive to win the vote. They insisted that if women were involved in politics, the world would be a more peaceful place.

But this did not go down well with many people. Sylvia Pankhurst was pelted with paint and rotten fruit by angry soldiers who objected to her peace meetings.

Pacifists – particularly pacifist men – were regarded with suspicion both by the government and the public during the First World War.

Most people believed that if a man was fit and healthy, he should do his duty and fight for his king and country. Women, of course, were not allowed to fight.

Men who refused to fight were called 'conscientious objectors'. They were also called cowards and shirkers, and often brutally beaten, shunned by friends and even family, and put in prison.

The Order of the White Feather MCMXIV

But being a conscientious objector did not mean a man was a coward or a shirker.

To be 'conscientious' means to be controlled by your own personal sense of what is right and wrong, and approximately 16,000 men refused to fight in the First World War, for religious or political reasons, or because they felt they could never kill another man.

On 30 August 1914, Admiral Charles Fitzgerald created what he called the Order of the White Feather and enlisted thirty women to help him.

A white feather was a traditional symbol of cowardice, and the practice of giving them to young men dressed in civilian clothing, rather than the khaki uniform of a serving soldier, quickly caught on. The idea was to shame them into joining the army.

Many more women, including some suffragettes, took on the role of presenting white feathers to men.

The feather would be placed in the man's hand, or tucked into the lapel of his jacket, always in a public place to cause him maximum humiliation. The whole process was extremely cruel. It targeted not only conscientious objectors, but also soldiers not in uniform, including those home on leave whose uniform was being cleaned from infestations of lice, or men who had been discharged from the army with disabling injuries sustained in battle.

It also became an embarrassing problem for men in occupations the government felt were too important for them to leave, such as miners or train and bus drivers. These men were issued with badges that read 'King and Country'. Likewise, men who had enlisted into the army but were waiting to be called up were issued with armbands to show they were soldiers in waiting, in order to avoid the inevitable shame of receiving a white feather.

Perhaps saddest of all were the young boys of fifteen and sixteen who just happened to look older than their age.

A man had to be eighteen years old to enlist in the army, but often when these boys were handed a white feather they felt so disgraced that they lied about their age and joined up immediately.

Feathers were even sent through the post, sometimes by a man's own family, with notes calling him a 'trench dodger' or a 'chicken heart'.

It is hard to imagine why so many women, including suffragettes, took to shaming men so horribly. Perhaps they felt they were being patriotic in giving out white feathers, because there was a real fear that if the army didn't have enough men to defend it, Britain would lose the war.

Indeed the government itself urged women to encourage men to join the army. They printed leaflets and posters using such manipulative language as: 'If your young man neglects his duty to his King and Country, the time will come when he will neglect you. Think it over – and then ask him to JOIN THE ARMY TODAY.'

Or maybe for the first time these women felt empowered to tell men what to do, having always been told what to do by men.

1915: For Men Must Fight and Women Must Work

AS WAR THUNDERED ON, MORE AND MORE MEN JOINED UP TO FIGHT, AND CONSEQUENTLY THE WORKFORCE, ESSENTIAL TO KEEP THE COUNTRY RUNNING, DWINDLED. THERE WAS AN URGENT NEED FOR WORKERS TO FILL THE JOBS LEFT OPEN BY THIS MASS EXODUS OF MEN.

There was no shortage of women willing and wanting to work, but employers were reluctant to give women the jobs previously exclusively occupied by men. They thought the war might be over soon and the men safely home. Besides, they believed women were probably not capable of taking on men's work.

This conundrum brought about a rather strange alliance between two former enemies.

The government were all too aware of the influence Emmeline Pankhurst had had in recruiting women to join the fight to win the vote. Might she be useful in the fight to win the war? The King himself asked the government if Mrs Pankhurst could be effective in showing the public that a workforce of women was a good idea.

Emmeline was given a grant of £2,000 by the government – a huge sum of money in 1915 – to organize a great parade of women. This time they would be marching not for the right to vote, but for the right to work and serve the country in its hour of great need.

Mrs Pankhurst was more than enthusiastic, and with the support of the WSPU the 'Women's War Work' demonstration was organized within two weeks.

On 17 July 1915, she led a procession of over 30,000 women and ninety marching bands through the streets of London in lashing rain and whipping wind. The women walked proudly, watched by over 100,000 spectators.

Unlike the previous marches and demonstrations organized by the WSPU, this time there were no green, white and purple flags or banners. Instead the marchers waved the red, white and blue of the Union Jack.

Tables had been set up along the route as recruitment stations where women could register their interest in working to help win the war. It was a great success, and women from all classes and backgrounds eagerly signed up.

In a speech to the assembled crowds, David Lloyd George, then the Government Minister of Munitions, spoke of the urgency of employing women in full-time work, particularly in the munitions factories. An army needs ammunition to be victorious. The women were pleased to help.

1915–1918: Canaries and Penguins Help Win the War

MAKING BOMBS IS HARD, HIGHLY SKILLED WORK, AND EXTREMELY DANGEROUS. BUT WOMEN WERE PREPARED TO TAKE THE RISKS.

Factories and employers had realized the need to employ women, and by the end of the war it is thought there were almost one million women working in munitions factories. These workers were called 'Munitionettes', and they played a crucial role in keeping the army supplied with bombs and bullets.

Alongside the risk of unplanned explosions, another serious hazard was poisoning by the chemicals used to make the explosives – including TNT, which turned their skin bright yellow and their hair green, and so earned them the nickname 'the Canaries'. Although these alarming symptoms wore off in time, other effects of working with such dangerous chemicals did result in the death of some women.

Some safety precautions were introduced, including face masks, protective clothing and wooden shoes.

A blow from anything metal could detonate the TNT, so there was a ban on all metal items being worn on the factory floor, such as hairpins or jewellery. And there were no matches allowed; a worker could be sent to jail for bringing a match to work. But accidents still happened.

Of course, working-class women had always worked, but now with so many men away fighting in the war, they had much wider opportunities available to them. This brought with it the chance to earn more money: by the end of the war, over 400,000 women had left low-paid domestic service to pursue other opportunities.

For the first time, women became police officers and fire fighters, railway porters and ticket collectors, carpenters and electricians, tram and bus conductors, even chimney sweeps and grave diggers – all jobs that had previously been thought of as exclusively 'men's work'.

The posh London department store Harrods employed several women as van drivers, commenting that they were 'good, careful drivers, who had few accidents and were much less tired at the end of the working day than the male drivers had been'.

But they didn't just drive the vehicles; they learned how to fix them, too: women became welders, mechanics and engineers.

Women also worked in agriculture: the Women's Land Army was formed in 1917 to provide the country with enough food to survive the war.

Nurses played a vital part in caring for soldiers both at home in Britain and overseas on the battlefields, where the fighting raged on around them. There were 3,000 nurses when war was declared, and 23,000 by the time it ended.

The VAD (Voluntary Aid Detachment) and the FANYS (First Aid Nursing Yeomanry) drove ambulances, ran hospitals and patched up the wounded.

The war also saw the first women join the Armed Forces – not to fight with the men, but to provide practical support. The WVR (Women's Volunteer Reserve) was founded in 1914, right at the start of the war.

The WAAC (Women's Auxiliary Army Corps), the WRNS (Women's Royal Naval Service) and the WRAF (Women's Royal Air Force) were all founded between 1917 and 1918.

The WRAF trained women to be air mechanics, but they were not allowed to actually fly the planes into war, which earned them the nickname 'the penguins' because they, like the birds, were 'flightless'. It would have been quite unthinkable in previous generations to see women in so many 'male' jobs, let alone in the Armed Forces, but the war offered these opportunities – and women were ready to take them.

Seeing women in these roles made the government's position against giving them the vote ever more ridiculous. As the headline of the suffragette newspaper *Votes for Women* put it in December 1915: 'Why Not Votes For Two As Well As Jobs For Two?' If a woman was as capable as a man of doing a job, surely she was as capable of voting.

1918: The Vote Won

VICTORY AT LAST! AFTER CAMPAIGNING FOR OVER SIXTY YEARS, WOMEN HAD FINALLY WON THE VOTE.

On 6 February 1918, the Representation of the People Act became law. All men over the age of twenty-one, then the age when someone was considered an adult, received the right to vote. Men in the military could vote at nineteen. This was the first time in British history that all men, regardless of wealth or status, were given political equality with each other.

But victory for women came with restrictions. To qualify to vote, a woman had to be over the age of thirty. In addition, she had to own her own home, or be married to a property owner. She also had the right to vote if she was a university graduate, or if she was paying an annual rent on a property of £5 or over.

Eight million women won the right to vote under the Representation of the People Act of 1918. But if women had been given full political equality with men, it would have meant that 21 million women would have been eligible to vote in the next parliamentary election.

There are many theories as to why the vote was given only to women over the age of thirty. Some historians believe the government still viewed younger women as too irresponsible to take voting seriously. Others believe that, because women outnumbered men, and the government had no idea how women would vote, politicians were afraid of making women the voting majority in case it favoured their opponents in the next general election.

Whatever the reason for not giving women full political equality with men in 1918, the government had recognized it could no longer ignore the idea of women's suffrage.

In 1916, when her focus was on winning the war rather than winning the vote, Emmeline Pankhurst was asked about the suffragettes' campaign and replied, 'We are like a dog that has buried a bone. They think we have forgotten all about it, but we've got the place marked.'

The government feared that when eventually the war came to an end, the suffragettes would reignite their militant actions with an even greater ferocity than they had before.

It was the war that had also highlighted the need to reform the voting qualifications for men.

Thousands of men were away from home, fighting for long periods of time. This effectively disenfranchised them (meaning that they were disallowed from voting) because a man had to have lived at his registered address for the previous twelve months in order to qualify to vote.

And then there were the millions of working-class soldiers who had no right to vote in the first place because they did not own property. These two things would have resulted in many men fighting for a country in which they could not vote. Such clear injustice could not be allowed to continue.

'Votes for Heroes' became a popular campaign to change this situation, and to this some suffragists added, 'Votes for Heroines, Too!'

Many believed that giving women the vote in 1918, albeit only to a select group, was the government's way of rewarding women for all their hard work and sacrifice during the Great War.

Although the Representation of the People Act was a monumental victory for the suffragists and suffragettes, there wasn't much of a mood for celebration. The war was still raging, and the casualties increasing.

War rumbled on for nine more months, until it finally came to an end on 11 November 1918.

Over 800,000 British men were dead, and thousands of others were horribly wounded.

It was in the aftermath of this horrific conflict that women first went to the polling stations to vote in the general election on 14 December 1918.

It was a victory for the women who had been fighting for so long, but only a partial victory. Equal voting rights with men was still a long way off, and the campaign continued for another ten years.

1928: Votes for All

EMMELINE PANKHURST DIED ON 14 JUNE 1928. JUST WEEKS LATER, THE EQUAL FRANCHISE ACT WAS MADE LAW, GIVING THE VOTE TO ALL WOMEN OVER THE AGE OF TWENTY-ONE.

Emmeline, after all her years tirelessly campaigning to win votes for women, did not live to see this victory. But Millicent Fawcett, then eighty-one years old, was invited to Parliament to witness the new Act pass into law. That evening she wrote in her diary: 'It is almost exactly sixty-one years ago since I heard John Stuart Mill introduce his (female) suffrage amendment to the Reform Bill on May 20th 1867, so I have had extraordinary good luck in having seen the struggle from the beginning.'

Five million more women became eligible to vote as a result of the Equal Franchise Act, which at 52.7 per cent, made women the voting majority over men.

There was not much opposition to the new law. Most people could see it was utter nonsense that women should be made to wait until they reached the age of thirty and met the appropriate property qualifications, when all men could vote from the age of twenty-one, or nineteen for men serving in the military. (The voting age was reduced to eighteen, for men and women, in 1969.)

When the Qualification of Women Act became law on 21 November 1918, women could stand for Parliament on equal terms with men, and become MPs. So women could stand for election between the ages of twenty-one and thirty – while not being able to vote themselves until they were older. Despite this ridiculous contradiction, seventeen women stood for election in 1918. They included the great pioneers Christabel Pankhurst, Emmeline Pethick-Lawrence and Charlotte Despard.

Only one woman standing for election that year was voted into Parliament. Constance Markievicz was elected to represent Dublin St Patrick's, making her the first woman to win a seat in the House of Commons. At the time, Ireland was still ruled from Westminster, but because of the political struggle for Irish independence, Constance never actually came to London to take up her seat in Parliament.

The following year, on 23 December 1919, the Sex Disqualification (Removal) Act became law. Professions and jobs that previously excluded women could no longer do so. This gave women access for the first time to careers as lawyers, accountants, magistrates, solicitors or civil servants.

By 1928, with women taking on increasingly important roles, and even becoming MPs, the country was more than ready for the long overdue Equal Franchise Act.

The general election of 1929 was the first in which women aged twenty-one to twenty-nine could vote. The number of female MPs rose to fourteen, and the Labour politician Margaret Bondfield became the first female Cabinet Minister.

Although women's place in society had taken a gigantic leap forward since the first Great People's Reform Act of 1832, the Equal Franchise Act of 1928 was still only one step towards balancing the many inequalities that still existed between women and men.

The fight for women's suffrage was a fight to win the parliamentary vote, but it was also about changing the view of women in society: not just how society viewed women, but how women viewed themselves.

The suffragists and suffragettes knew that by putting women at the very heart of politics, and giving women a political voice, they could change the old repressive, discriminatory perceptions of women and femininity and strive to achieve real gender equality.

The battle for full equality continues today, but through their tenacity and fearless determination, the tireless campaigners for women's suffrage had won a hugely important victory – for themselves, and for the generations that followed.

A World of Suffrage

ALL OVER THE WORLD, WOMEN HAVE HAD TO FIGHT WITH BRAVERY AND DETERMINATION FOR THEIR RIGHT TO A PARLIAMENTARY VOTE.

SOJOURNER TRUTH (1797–1883)

Sojourner Truth was an American civil rights campaigner and an early supporter of women's equality. She was born into slavery as Isabella Baumfree, one of a large family from whom she was separated at the age of nine, when she was sold for the first of three times.

In 1826, her owner John Dumont promised to free Isabella, but he broke his promise, and so instead she fled with her young daughter to a local family who supported the abolition of slavery and bought her freedom. Shortly after this, she learned that her son, Peter, then only five years old, had been illegally sold. Isabella went to court to get him back –

'Truth is powerful and it prevails.'

and won. The case became one of the first in which a black woman successfully challenged a white man in America.

In 1843 Isabella changed her name to Sojourner Truth and, fired by her personal experience of slavery, began campaigning for civil rights – for all people to be treated equally, regardless of colour or race. She also became a powerful spokesperson for women's rights and suffrage. In what became known as her 'Ain't I a Woman?' speech of 1851, she said that women deserved equal rights with men because they were equally capable and could 'plough, reap, husk and chop' as any man could.

She wanted political equality for *all* women, but at the time the anti-slavery movement was focused only on the rights of black men and not on those of black women. Sojourner believed that once black *men* received the vote, the fight for women's suffrage, both black and white, would fade. In a way she was right. Women's suffrage was not won in America until 1920, fifty years after the law was passed that allowed all men, regardless of race or colour, the right to vote. Sojourner herself had died some ten years earlier, but she had continued campaigning well into old age.

'Failure is impossible.'

SUSAN B. ANTHONY (1820–1906)

A teacher and civil rights campaigner, Susan was a co-founder of both the American Equal Rights Association and the National Woman Suffrage Association, and appeared before every US government between 1869 and 1906 demanding votes for women. She voted illegally in the presidential election of 1872 and was arrested, along with the election inspectors who had allowed her to vote, and fined the then substantial sum of $100. She did not live to see women finally get the vote in 1920, but the law became known as the Susan B. Anthony Amendment, acknowledging her tireless fight for women's rights.

'The way to right wrongs is to turn the light of truth upon them.'

IDA B. WELLS (1862–1931)

A journalist and civil rights campaigner, Ida was only twenty-two when she sued the train company that refused her a seat in a whites-only 'ladies' carriage. She later founded the first black woman's suffrage association in America, the Alpha Suffrage Club. In 1913, at a woman's suffrage march in Washington, she refused to walk at the back where the African American women had been told to go. Instead Ida marched at the front alongside the white suffragists, raising awareness of how women of colour were often overlooked within the suffrage campaign.

MERI TE TAI MANGAKAHIA (1868–1920)
A campaigner for women's suffrage in New Zealand, she was the first woman to address the Maori political assembly, asking that women be allowed to vote for, and stand as, members of the Maori parliament.

BRÍET BJARNHÉÐINSDÓTTIR (1856–1940)
An early supporter of women's liberation, she was the first Icelandic woman to write a newspaper article (on women's rights). She founded Iceland's first women's magazine, and the first women's suffrage society.

FUSAE ICHIKAWA (1893–1981)
A teacher and journalist who later became a politician, she was a keen women's suffrage supporter. In 1918 she organized the New Woman's Association, and in 1924 founded the Women's Suffrage League of Japan.

SAROJINI NAIDU (1879–1949)
The first Indian women to be president of the Indian National Congress, she was called the 'Nightingale of India' for the beautiful poetry she wrote. She helped found the Women's India Association in 1917.

LIN ZONGSU (1878–1944)
She formed the Women's Suffrage Comrades Alliance in 1911, the first organization of its kind in China, and established a journal, *Women's Time*, to publish information about suffrage.

DORIA SHAFIK (1908–1975)
A principal leader of the Egyptian women's liberation movement, she published a magazine focusing on women's issues in order to encourage Egyptian women to have an effective role within society.

MEENA KESHWAR KAMAL (1956–1987)
While still a student she established the Revolutionary Association of the Women of Afghanistan to help promote equality for women, and later founded the bilingual magazine *Women's Message*.

MELITTA MARXER (1923–2015)
In 1968 she formed the Committee for Women's Suffrage in Liechtenstein. In 1983, she and others spoke in front of the Council of Europe, bringing the international spotlight to their fight.

The battle for women's suffrage worldwide has a long and complicated history. The dates beside each country show when women were first allowed to vote there, but remember that, just as in the UK, many countries placed restrictions on who could vote, so the dates may not indicate the grant of full suffrage. Where possible, I have indicated when the suffrage granted was only partial.

1881: Isle of Man (partial)
1893: New Zealand
1902: Australia (partial: not extended to Aboriginal people)
1906: Finland
1907: Norway (partial)
1908: Denmark (partial)
1913: Norway (full)
1915: Denmark (full)
1915: Iceland (partial)
1916: Canada (partial)
1917: Russia
1918: Austria
1918: Estonia
1918: Hungary
1918: Ireland (partial)
1918: Kyrgyzstan
1918: Latvia
1918: Poland
1918: United Kingdom (partial)
1919: Belarus
1919: Belgium (partial)
1919: Georgia
1919: Germany
1919: Luxembourg
1919: Netherlands
1919: Sweden
1919: Ukraine
1920: Albania
1920: Czech Republic
1920: Iceland (full)
1920: Lithuania
1920: Slovakia
1920: United States of America
1921: Armenia
1921: Azerbaijan
1922: Ireland (full)
1924: Ecuador
1924: Kazakhstan
1924: Mongolia
1924: Tajikistan
1925: Italy (partial)
1927: Turkmenistan
1928: United Kingdom (full)
1929: Puerto Rico (partial)
1929: Romania (partial)
1930: South Africa (partial)
1930: Turkey
1931: Chile (partial)
1931: Portugal (partial)
1931: Spain
1931: Sri Lanka
1932: Brazil
1932: Thailand
1932: Uruguay
1935: Myanmar
1935: Puerto Rico (full)

1937: Philippines
1938: Bolivia (partial)
1938: Uzbekistan
1939: El Salvador
1940: Cuba
1941: Panama (partial)
1942: Dominican Republic
1944: Bermuda (partial)
1944: Bulgaria
1944: Croatia
1944: France
1944: Jamaica
1945: Indonesia
1945: Italy (full)
1945: Japan
1945: Senegal
1945: Slovenia
1945: Togo
1945: Trinidad and Tobago
1946: Cameroon
1946: Democratic People's Republic of Korea (North Korea)
1946: Djibouti
1946: Guatemala
1946: Liberia
1946: Macedonia
1946: Montenegro
1946: Panama (full)
1946: Romania (full)
1946: Serbia
1946: Venezuela
1946: Vietnam
1947: Argentina
1947: India
1947: Malta
1947: Pakistan
1947: Singapore
1947: Taiwan
1947: Tuvalu
1948: Belgium (full)
1948: Israel
1948: Niger
1948: Republic of Korea (South Korea)
1948: Seychelles
1948: Suriname
1949: Bosnia and Herzegovina
1949: Chile (full)
1949: China
1949: Costa Rica
1949: Syria (partial)
1950: Barbados
1950: Haiti
1951: Antigua and Barbuda
1951: Dominica
1951: Grenada
1951: Nepal
1951: Saint Kitts and Nevis

1951: Saint Vincent and the Grenadines
1952: Bolivia
1952: Côte d'Ivoire
1952: Greece
1952: Lebanon
1953: Bhutan
1953: British Guiana
1953: Mexico (full)
1953: Syria (full)
1954: Belize
1954: Colombia
1954: Ghana
1954: Saint Lucia
1955: Cambodia
1955: Eritrea
1955: Ethiopia
1955: Honduras
1955: Nicaragua
1955: Peru
1956: Benin
1956: Comoros
1956: Egypt
1956: Gabon
1956: Mali
1956: Mauritius
1956: Somalia
1957: Malaysia
1957: Zimbabwe
1958: Burkina Faso
1958: Chad
1958: Guinea
1958: Laos
1958: Nigeria (partial)
1959: Brunei (there have been no voting rights for men or women since 1962)
1959: Madagascar
1959: San Marino
1959: Tanzania
1959: Tunisia
1960: Cyprus
1960: Gambia
1960: Tonga
1961: Burundi
1961: Malawi
1961: Mauritania
1961: Paraguay
1961: Rwanda
1961: Sierra Leone
1962: Algeria
1962: Australia (extended to Aboriginal people)
1962: Bahamas
1962: Monaco

1962: Uganda
1962: Zambia
1963: Congo (Republic)
1963: Equatorial Guinea
1963: Fiji
1963: Iran
1963: Kenya
1963: Morocco
1964: Afghanistan
1964: Libya
1964: Maldives
1964: Papua New Guinea
1964: Sudan (and since 2011, South Sudan)
1965: Botswana
1965: Lesotho
1967: Democratic Republic of the Congo (formerly Zaire)
1967: Kiribati
1967: People's Democratic Republic of Yemen (South Yemen)
1968: Bermuda (full)
1968: Nauru
1968: Swaziland
1970: Andorra
1970: Yemen Arab Republic (North Yemen)
1971: Switzerland
1972: Bangladesh
1973: Bahrain (no elections held until 2002)
1974: Jordan
1974: Solomon Islands
1975: Angola
1975: Cape Verde
1975: Mozambique
1975: Sao Tome and Principe
1975: Vanuatu
1976: Nigeria (full)
1976: Portugal (full)
1977: Guinea-Bissau
1978: Moldova
1979: Marshall Islands
1979: Micronesia
1979: Palau
1980: Iraq
1984: Liechtenstein
1986: Central African Republic
1989: Namibia
1990: Samoa
1994: South Africa (full)
1999: Qatar
2002: East Timor
2003: Oman
2005: Kuwait
2006: United Arab Emirates
2015: Saudi Arabia

VOTES FOR WOMEN